Fly Fishing Basics

Other Stackpole books by Dave Hughes

Handbook of Hatches
Reading the Water
Tackle & Technique for Taking Trout
Tactics for Trout
Strategies for Stillwater

FLY FISHING BASICS

David Hughes

Illustrated by
Richard Bunse

STACKPOLE
BOOKS

Published by
STACKPOLE BOOKS
5067 Ritter Road
Mechanicsburg, PA 17055
www.stackpolebooks.com

Printed in the United States of America

10   9

First edition

Cover illustration by Richard Bunse
Cover design by Caroline Miller

Library of Congress Cataloging-in-Publication Data

Hughes, Dave.
    Fly fishing basics / by Dave Hughes: illustrated by Richard Bunse.
      p.   cm.
    Includes bibliographical references (p.) and index.
    ISBN 0-8117-2439-5
    1. Fly fishing. I. Title
    SH456.H84   1994
    799.1'2-20

    ISBN 978-0-8117-2439-5

Contents

Chapter 1

Why Fly Fish?

Fly fishing is distinguished from other forms of fishing by some simple things such as grace and beauty. But the biggest difference is the one most often overlooked: efficiency. We think about fly fishing in terms of difficulty, but the truth is that once you learn to fish with flies, which is not nearly as difficult as it's often thought to be, you can commonly catch more fish by fly fishing than you can by any other method.

Why? The reasons, like the sport, are simple. First, many of the foods that fish eat are small and of a slight weight. You can cast imitations of these with a fly rod. You cannot cast them with any other type of gear.

Second, only a small part of every cast places a lure or fly in the most likely area to be taken by a fish: the two to three feet at the edge of some cover, or in the rings of a rise. The largest part of most retrieves is wasted. With other types of gear you've got to reel the lure all the way back to the rod tip before casting again. With fly gear you simply loft the fly at long range, as soon as it's out of the strike zone, and settle it instantly back to where fish are eager to whack it.

Still, despite the inherent effectiveness of fly fishing, don't ever overlook the importance of beauty and grace. There is something soothing about watching the weaving motions of the fly rod, the line glinting in loops in the air, the swift descent and soft arrival of the fly on the water. It is most interesting to watch when that landing gets punctuated by the detonation of a fish on the fly.

The pleasure of the spectator is nothing, however, when compared to the pleasure of the creator. The greatest happiness goes to the person who weaves those loops of line in the air, who orchestrates the events that cause that detonation. No other gear can give you the same magical sense of both mastery and mystery. You hold the rod in your hand, and it does such wonderful things to the line and fly that even you are not sure how you caused them to happen.

There is a final and fateful beauty in the places where fly fishing takes you: forested brooks, hidden lakes, trout streams, the seashore. It will take you wherever you want. It's one of the great mysteries of the sport that once you take it up you seem directed to some secret destination of your own, apart from the places all others go. Fly fishing is a journey on a long and wonderful path. Once you start, you'll never turn back.

Please come along.

COLDWATER FLY ROD FISH

Trout are the perfect fly rod fish for several reasons. Their foods, primarily insects and small crustaceans, are the right size to imitate with flies. The way trout feed, generally on the surface or in shallow water, makes it easy to deliver flies where trout will get a chance to take them. The small creeks, streams, and rivers where trout live most often keep them within easy casting range of your flies. When they live in larger rivers and in lakes, it's still easy to stalk into range to reach them with flies.

Other coldwater species that can often be tricked with flies include the steelhead, which is an ocean-going form of the rainbow trout, and both Atlantic and Pacific salmon.

Steelhead from 3 to 30 pounds enter streams from the Pacific Ocean or the Great Lakes in summer or in winter, though there are also minor runs of both spring and fall strains. The summer steelhead is an active fish, free-ranging and full of fight. When conditions are right it can be coaxed easily into rising upward and striking a fly that is fished either slightly sunk or right on the surface itself. Winter steelhead are less ambitious. To tempt them, you've usually got to get your fly right down to the bottom.

Atlantic salmon are considered by many to be the ultimate fly rod fish. They return from the Atlantic Ocean through spring, summer, and into fall. They weigh up to 40 or even 50 pounds, though you'd be foolish to be unhappy if you caught one that weighed over 15 to 20. They are active, and strike sunk or surface flies with determined thuds.

Pacific salmon, commonly either chinook (kings) or coho (silvers), are less often considered fly rod fish, though more folks are finding them catchable in their native Pacific coast waters and where they've been transplanted into the Great Lakes states. These salmon grow to whopping sizes, and sometimes take flies aggressively, though almost always down along the bottom.

WARMWATER FLY ROD FISH

Bass top the list of warmwater fish. Largemouth are the most widespread and sought-after of the bass species. They are often thought of as southern fish, because they thrive and reach their largest sizes in the warm belt of the southern states and northern Mexico. But they have migrated to many states, and have been planted in all the others. So they have expanded into excellent fly fishing populations in almost every state.

Largemouth bass are ruthless predators and feed rather recklessly on whatever swims, crawls, or creeps into range of their giant jaws. They take snakes, baby ducks, frogs, mice, crayfish, aquatic insects, and of course smaller fish, including each other. They are more adventurous than trout; the flies you cast to them need not resemble in any way a food form that they've ever encountered. If it looks like it might be good to eat, largemouth bass will be glad to try it out. They can be taken with topwater poppers, mid-water streamers, and deepwater sliders, along with most anything else you care to cast to them.

Smallmouth bass live more often in colder lakes, at slightly higher elevations or more northern latitudes than those preferred by largemouth. They are also found in moving water, though the streams they prefer are typically a bit warmer and slightly slower than those preferred by trout. Like largemouth, they feed on whatever they encounter and can ingest. But their environments tend to be more restricted in terms of the food forms that they offer to the fish, and smallmouth bass are more likely to be fooled into taking something that looks like a crayfish, minnow, or aquatic insect nymph or larva.

Bluegill, crappie, and other panfish are the perfect warmwater fly rod fish. Their natural foods, like those of the trout, are best imitated with flies, though it would be stretching it to say that they require that the flies fished for them be imitations of anything. If a fly is fished at the correct depth, so that it tiptoes through a school of panfish, and if it is small enough so that they can get it into their mouths, they'll accept almost anything.

3

FOODS THAT FLIES IMITATE

Flies can be purchased, or you can tie them yourself, to represent a wide range of the food forms that various fish species make a living eating. It's rarely necessary to fish exact imitations. As we've already seen, bass and lots of other fish are quite willing to experiment, to take flies that look like nothing they've ever seen. Fish are predators, however, and you're going to catch more of them if you show them flies that look at least a little like their most common prey, and use retrieves that cause the flies to act like that common prey form.

Fly fishing is so successful because flies can be tied and fished to look like submerged or floating insects, like various forms of baitfish, like frogs, mice, or like any other creature you can imagine and can wrap materials around a hook to resemble. Some saltwater flies are tied to look like scuttling crabs.

One of the largest trout this author has ever caught, a fiercely predaceous bull trout that weighed some six pounds, fell to a fly—a rather large and ungainly one!—tied to imitate a ten-inch hatchery trout.

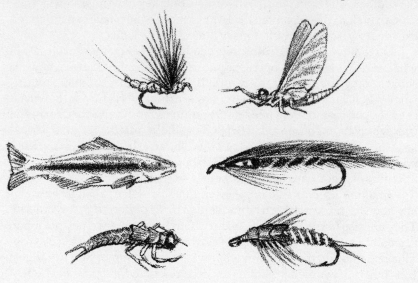

Chapter 2
Basic Fly Fishing Tackle

At its simplest, fly fishing requires just five items: rod, reel, line, leader, and fly. Of course, it's never left to rest at that level. But these five elements are at the heart of fly fishing and make up the basic fly fishing outfit. They are the first things you'll want to trot out and buy.

Your outfit selection should follow a logical progression. The size of the foods eaten by the fish species you're after dictates the size flies you'll need to cast. The size of those flies dictates the weight of the line that you'll need to lift them into the air and carry them gracefully. The weight of the chosen fly line dictates the stiffness and strength of the rod you'll need in order to cast it, and also dictates the size of the reel you'll need to hold it. The leader must transfer the energy of the cast from a certain weight line to a specific size fly.

We almost always select a rod first, then choose lines and reels to fit it. But it's the fly line, and not the rod, that is at the core of outfit selection. Decide on the line weight first, then select a rod that will propel it.

The best advice you can get, when setting out to purchase a first outfit, is to ask a more experienced fly fishing friend to go with you. Find a specialized fly fishing shop or a sporting goods store that has a broad selection of fly fishing tackle, and listen carefully to what your mentor has to tell you.

The second best advice is to go to a fly fishing shop and depend on the shop clerk for advice. But be very careful to explain your level of experience or lack of it. And be sure to explain to the clerk what kind of water you intend to fish, and what kind of fish you intend to pursue with your new outfit, or he'll outfit you for something he'd like to do himself.

The secret is to decide what you're going to fish for and where you're going to fish for it. Then go out and buy equipment that suits the fish species and its situation.

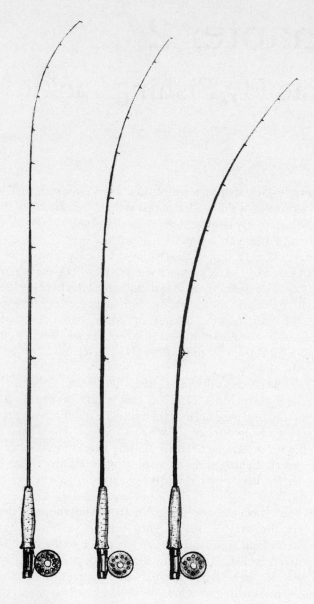

FLY ROD SELECTION

Your first rod should be a modestly priced graphite suited best to the kind of fishing you intend to do most often. Don't buy a cheap one; it won't offer much but difficulty as you begin learning to cast. Don't buy a fiberglass rod; for the most part graphite rods are lighter and more responsive. Don't buy bamboo; you might graduate to one of those later, but they are very expensive, and your money is better spent elsewhere at first.

Rod Length.

Short rods, 6½ to 7½ feet, are best for small streams, where the problems you encounter will be brush overhead. Long rods, 9½ to 10½ feet, are best for the largest of rivers, where you need the maximum loft for line control. Medium-length rods, 8 to 9 feet long, fish over the widest range of situations, and therefore are the most useful. They are also least critical of casting mistakes, hence the easiest on which to learn.

Rod Action.

Fly rods are classed as *slow, medium, or fast.* A medium to medium-fast action is best for the beginner, and in the long run (as they slowly discover after trying other actions), also best for most experienced fly fishermen.

Rod Line Weight.

Rods are designed to cast a specific line weight, though many will serve for a line weight one size heavier or lighter. Be sure to choose a rod to cast the size line that suits the range of fish sizes you're after.

Basic Outfit.

Assuming it suits what you're after, which it most often will, the best beginning outfit is an 8½ to 9 foot rod balanced to a double taper 5- or 6-weight line. It will serve as an excellent learning outfit. You'll also find it at the center of your needs over a long span of years. An 8½ foot rod for a 5-weight line is the first outfit this author reaches for on about 90 percent of his fishing trips today.

ROD AND LINE-WEIGHT PURPOSES

1-, 2-, 3-weight:	Light trout or panfish in windless conditions.
4-, 5-, 6-weight:	Trout in average situations; light bass.
7-, 8-, 9-weight:	Heavy trout; bass; salmon/steelhead; light saltwater.
10-, 11-, 12-weight:	Average to heavy saltwater.

THE THREE-ROD BATTERY

Always select your first basic outfit for the kind of fishing you intend to do *most often*. Don't buy a compromise outfit if you plan to fish for trout on the smallest of streams, with occasional excursions on other waters. Instead, buy the right light outfit for just such fishing, and make it work as well as you can when you want to do something else. That way you won't be fishing constantly with the wrong gear when you're fishing the waters you love to fish best.

The same applies if you love to pound lily pads with big bass poppers. Get an outfit that does it well. Make that outfit compromise for everything else, or get another outfit when the need arises often enough to justify it.

Select your quarry first, the tackle to fish for it second.

When African hunters used to go on safari, they selected three rifles, a light, a medium, and a heavy, for the different weights of game. It's an idea that can be applied to fly fishing. It will help you select the outfit that applies best to the kind of fishing you do most often. It will also help you decide what a good second, and then third, outfit might be. If you complete the battery of three outfits over time, you'll be equipped for all manner of fishing in your future.

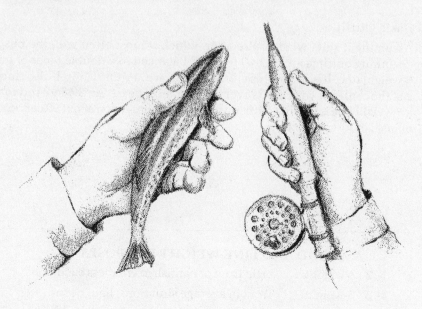

The Light.

If you're primarily going to be fishing for panfish and trout, using small flies and desiring delicate presentations, then choose an 8 to 9 foot rod that propels a 4- or 5-weight line.

The Medium.

If you'll primarily be fishing for trout in big rivers or on lakes, or you're going to be after bass and other fish of similar size with modest size flies, choose an 8½ to 9½ foot rod for a 6- or 7-weight line.

The Heavy.

If your quarry will be big trout, fished for with big weighted flies, or you'll want to cast large flies for bass, then choose an 8½ to 9½ foot rod for an 8- or 9-weight line. The same outfit will be perfect for salmon and steelhead fishing.

Specialty Rods.

Other rods fit at the ends of the spectrum, and fish only in limited situations. Rods for 1-, 2-, and 3-weight lines are useful with tiny flies, on windless days. Rods for 10-, 11-, and 12-weight lines are useful for tarpon and other large saltwater quarry.

FLY REELS

Reels aren't as critical in fly fishing as in other kinds of fishing. The reel is used to store the line between casts, but not to cast or to retrieve the lure. However, the reel is also used to play strong fish, so if you're after any but the smallest fish, say tiny trout and also panfish, it's best to get a reel with a smooth and dependable drag.

A simple click drag, or spring-and-paul mechanism, will be good enough for most trout, bass, and other medium-sized fish. If you're going after steelhead, salmon, and saltwater fish, the reel becomes much more important, and it's best to get one with a high-quality disc drag. For these kinds of fishing, it's not a mistake to spend more on the reel than you do for the rod.

Automatic reels are all right if you know you are never going to play a fish that will be strong enough, or run fast and far enough, to take line off the reel. You simply cannot give line to a fish with an automatic. They're also too heavy for all but the stoutest of rods. It's best to avoid automatics, although they have their fans among small stream trout fishermen, and also among those who fish for panfish and bass.

Single-action reels are the most common kind, and the most useful. They store the line efficiently. They also give up line gracefully to the run of a fish. They have few moving parts, and little that can go wrong. The spool turns a single time with each revolution of the handle, hence the name single-action.

Double-action reels revolve two to three times with each turn of the handle, thus increasing the rate of retrieve. This is handy when fighting fish that make long runs. But, fish taken while fishing with double-action reels, for obscure reasons, are not considered to be taken while fly fishing. Hence they are not qualified for the record books.

Single-action reels are generally the best buy and the best way to go, with spring-and-paul drags for trout, bass, and panfish, and with more expensive but stronger disc drags for salmon, steelhead, and saltwater fishing.

The reel should be big enough to handle all of the chosen fly line plus enough Dacron backing line to ensure you won't run out of line when a fish makes a long run. That means 50 to 100 yards of backing for trout, 150 to 200 yards for steelhead and salmon, and 200 to 300 yards for saltwater fish. Be sure to consider space for the backing when buying a reel.

You'll usually want to carry an extra line or two in different sink rates for various fishing situations. So you'll want the option of using spare spools. When you purchase a reel, be sure that extra spools are available for it. They're cheaper than buying a separate reel for each line, and they also take up less room in the fishing vest.

FLY LINES

Fly Line Weight.

A fly by itself is too light to cast. The fly line provides the weight for the cast. Its weight loads the rod. The weight of it turning over in the air, on the forecast, carries the fly to where you want it.

The line weight must be in balance with the stiffness of the rod. If it's too light, it won't load the rod, and you won't be able to cast it. If it's too heavy, it will overload the rod and kill the cast. Rods are rated for a specific line size, but some will cast one size lighter or heavier.

STANDARD FLY LINE WEIGHTS FOR FIRST 30 FEET			
#1	60 grains	#7	185 grains
#2	80 grains	#8	210 grains
#3	100 grains	#9	240 grains
#4	120 grains	#10	280 grains
#5	140 grains	#11	330 grains
#6	160 grains	#12	380 grains

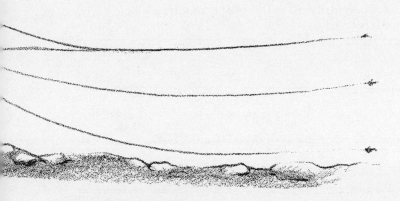

LINE SINK RATES

A *floating line* is the most useful line of all. With it you can fish dry flies on top, wet flies and streamers just under the surface, and weighted nymphs down to 4 or 5 feet deep. An *intermediate line* is used most often when fishing lakes, with flies suspended a few inches deep. It hangs just below the surface, and is removed from the effects of wind and waves.

The *slow sinking line* is useful for getting a fly down a foot or two. A *fast sinking line* will deliver a fly down 5 to 10 feet in still water, or 2 to 3 feet in fast water. It is perhaps the most useful of sinking lines. The *extra-fast sinking line* is designed to deliver your fly down 10′ and 20′. In lakes you can count it down to depths that you could not otherwise fish. In streams it will cut a heavy current and get your fly down to where large fish often hold in deep pools.

Lead-core lines are usually 20 to 25 foot shooting heads. They are the ultimate for reaching the depths, and quickly. They are used most often in specialty fishing: for salmon, steelhead, or in saltwater.

FLY LINE TAPERS

A line is rated according to the weight in the first 30 ft. Rods are nearly always rated to cast double-taper lines. If you choose another taper, it's usually necessary to buy one line weight heavier. In other words, if a rod casts best with a 5-weight, then it will probably require a weight-forward 6-weight to load it properly.

Level Line.

Cheap, but best to avoid. It has no front taper to allow soft delivery of a fly.

Double-Taper.

Excellent choice for the floating line you'll use most. It allows delicate casts, is fair for distance, and gives you excellent line control in the air and on the water.

Weight-Forward.

The first choice when your goal is distance. Its casting weight is in the first 30'. It does have a front taper and can be cast softly at short range.

Triangle Taper.

A *Lee Wulff* line. Its long front taper allows delicate casts; good for distance, excellent for roll casting.

Long Belly.

Longer front taper and longer belly than weight-forward. Good for distance, fair for delicacy and control.

Shooting Head.

Just 30′ of fly line looped to thin running line. Designed for distance or a quick switch of sink rates.

FLY LINE NOMENCLATURE AND BACKING LINE

Fly Line Nomenclature.

Fly lines are labeled for their taper, weight, and whether they are sinking or floating. A double-taper is DT; a weight-forward is WF. A floating line is F; a sinking line is S; a combination floating/sinking line is F/S. A double-taper, 6-weight, floating line is labeled DT6F. A weight-forward, 5-weight, sinking line is a WF5S. It's simple. A weight-forward 7-weight line with a 10′ fast sinking wet-tip is labeled WF7F/S 10′ Fast-Sink Wet-tip.

EXAMPLES OF FLY LINE NOMENCLATURE

DT4F:	double-taper, 4-weight, floating.
WF8S:	weight-forward, 8-weight, sinking.
TT6F:	triangle taper, 6-weight, floating.
SH7S:	shooting head, 7-weight, sinking.
WF9F/S 20′ Wet-Belly Fast-Sinking:	weight-forward, 9-weight, floating/sinking line with a 20′ fast sinking portion.

Backing Line.

A fly line is only 90′ to 105′ long. If you hook a fish strong enough to run it all out, you've got to have backing line on the reel behind the fly line so the fish can keep going without breaking off. Your backing should be thin woven Dacron of twenty- or thirty-pound test. Do not use monofilament; it compresses on the reel spool, then expands and jams the reel.

For panfish, you don't need backing. For trout and bass, it's a good idea to have 50 to 100 yards of 20# backing. For steelhead and salmon, you need 100 to 150 yards of 20# or 30# backing. In saltwater, bonefish and tarpon and many other species are known for their long first runs. Your reel should hold 300 yards of 30# backing.

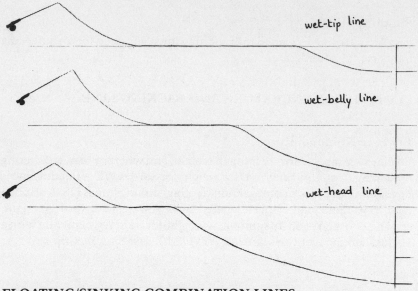

wet-tip line

wet-belly line

wet-head line

FLOATING/SINKING COMBINATION LINES

The most popular and most useful sinking lines do not sink over the entire length of line. Instead, they sink only in the front few feet, and the rest floats. This combination of floating/sinking portions has major advantages: the sinking part takes the fly down where you want it, but the remainder stays up on the surface where you can see it and control it.

Floating/sinking combinations come in all the range of sink rates mentioned earlier: slow, fast, and extra-fast sinking. They come in wet-tip, wet-belly, and wet-head formulations.

Wet-Tip.

The first 10′ of the line sinks, the rest floats. Purchased in a fast or extra-fast sink rate, this line lets you fish from 2′ to 8′ down, depending on the speed of the current.

Wet-Belly.

The first 20′ sinks. In fast or extra-fast sinking, it gets the fly down 8′ to 12′ in slow pools and stillwaters. It also allows a retrieve that does not lift the fly in the water as it is drawn toward the rod.

Wet-Head.

The first 30′ sinks, the rest floats. In fast or extra-fast sinking, it gets the fly down 12′ to 20′ in stillwaters or pools. It keeps the fly deep during most of the retrieve, rather than lifting it up toward the rod.

FLY LINE CARE AND FLY LINE COLOR

Fly Line Care.

Modern fly lines need little care, when compared to old silk lines that needed to be dried and then dressed between fishing trips. Most folks now make the mistake of thinking that fly lines need no care at all—which is far from true.

All fly lines pick up microscopic bits of dirt from the water. When dirty, they no longer shoot cleanly through the guides, and this shortens the cast. Floating lines begin to sink; sinking lines fail to sink at their designated rate.

All fly lines should be cleaned at least once a day. Floating lines should be dressed with line cleaner and floatant before you begin fishing each day. Run a floatant pad over the line two to four times, stretching the line as you do. If the line gets dirty during the day, clean and dress it again. Run sinking lines through a wetted handkerchief; do not apply floatant.

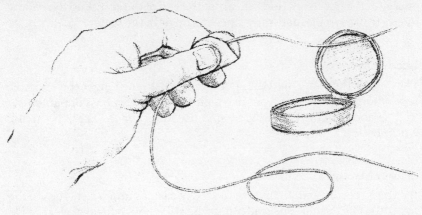

Fly Line Color.

Color is not as important as most folks suppose. If a line goes over a fish, the fish will see it no matter what its color. It's best to select a color that you can see well for your floating line; orange, yellow, lime green, peach, or ivory are all the same to the trout.

Sinking lines and sinking tips get down where fish can see them, so they're nearly always a dark color, to be less noticeable. That's the way it should be.

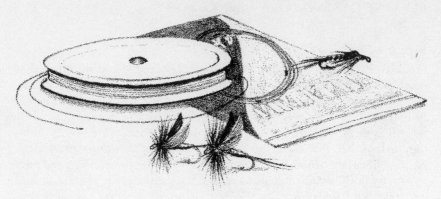

LEADERS

Leaders serve three functions in fly fishing. They separate the thick line from the fly with a connection that is, in theory, invisible. They transfer the energy of the line to turn over the fly at the end of the cast. And they allow the fly to drift freely, naturally, once it's on or in the water.

Leader Length.

The calmer the water, and the spookier the fish, the longer the invisible separation you need. For trout in rough water, and for bass or panfish, 7′ to 9′ is about right. For trout in smooth water, or in lakes, 10′ to 14′ works better.

Leader Strength.

This must correspond to the size of the fly cast, as much as it does to the size of the fish caught. The leader must be stiff enough to turn over the fly, but also be fine enough to give a dry fly or nymph a free drift.

Leader Taper.

To transfer energy from the line to the fly, the leader must be stout at the butt, thinner through the middle, then have a long and fine front end, called the *tippet*. Tapered leaders can be tied of ever-finer sections knotted together, or they can be bought knotless, with the taper built in.

The "X"System.

In the old days of silkworm gut leaders, this natural material was extruded through fine holes to elongate it into leader sections that were then tied together. A 5X leader section was extruded five times, thus was much finer than a 3X section, extruded only three times.

Modern leaders are still rated by the "X" system, but it now refers to the leader diameter in thousandths of an inch (see the chart that follows). A 5X leader is .006 in., a 3X is .008 in. It makes more sense to refer to the diameter than it does to the "X" rating of a leader. Both are now printed on leader spools. But those of us old enough to have first learned the earlier "X" system still use it. Most fly fishermen learn it and use it to refer to their tippets to this day.

LEADER DIMENSIONS

"X"	Diameter	Fly Size	Approx. Pound Test
0X	.011″	1/0, 1, 2	6½ to 15½
1X	.010″	4, 6, 8	5½ to 13½
2X	.009″	6, 8, 10	4½ to 11½
3X	.008″	10, 12, 14	4 to 8½
4X	.007″	12, 14, 16	3 to 6½
5X	.006″	14, 16, 18, 20	2½ to 4½
6X	.005″	18, 20, 22, 24	1½ to 3½
7X	.004″	20, 22, 24, 26	1 to 3
8X	.003″	22, 24, 26, 28	¾ to 1¾

Not all leaders of the same diameter are the same strength, which is why fly leaders are referred to by diameter rather than pound test. Manufacturers vary a lot. Because leader brands vary in strength and in relative stiffness or limpness, you should never tie two different brands together. Choose a brand, and stick with it.

LEADER TIPS

Leaders Simplified.
Buy a few basic knotless leaders in two lengths, for example 7½' and 10', and always carry them in your vest. Make them one size stouter than you would normally use, for example 2X or 3X if you usually fish 4X or 5X for size 12 to 16 flies. Then buy and carry spools of the most commonly used tippets, say 4X, 5X, and 6X, in the same brand material. When you get to the lake or stream and choose a fly to tie on, add the appropriate length and diameter tippet to the basic leader for that fly and situation. This simplified process prepares you to meet nearly any fly fishing situation with a minimum of mass to carry.

Leader Length.
For most dry, wet, nymph, and streamer fishing, a leader the length of your rod or a bit longer will be about perfect. That translates to a leader between 8½' and 10'.

Far and Fine.
When fishing small dry flies over rising trout, on smooth water, use a leader that is 10' to 14' long, with the fine tippet 2' to 4' of that length.

Tippet Length.
14" tippets were once recommended because that was as long as gut could be extruded. With modern monofilaments, use tippets about 2' long for most fishing, but 3' to 4' if you're fishing over fussy trout. If the leader gets cut back to 15" or so as you change flies during the day, then take time to tie on a new tippet that is the original length.

Wind Problems.
If the wind bosses your fly and your leader around, and you can't get the fly to go where you want it, shorten your leader and go up one size in your tippet. In windy conditions, fish are less leader shy anyway. Casting control becomes more important than delicacy.

KNOTS

Though you can certainly learn a Gordian tangle of knots, five basic knots will serve all but the rarest of fly fishing needs. You need to know the simple *backing knot* to attach your line to the reel. The *surgeon's knot* is a useful leader-to-leader and tippet knot, especially when the segments are more than two thousandths of an inch different in diameter. The *blood knot* is the more common leader-to-leader knot. The *nail knot* is used to attach backing to the rear of the line, and a leader to the front. The *improved clinch knot* affixes a fly to the tippet.

Backing Knot.

Loop backing around reel spindle. Tie overhand knot around backing line, then another overhand knot in tag end. Draw both down tight, then snug against the spindle.

Surgeon's Knot.

Overlap leader ends 3″-5″. Make overhand knot, pull tag ends through. Repeat. Moisten knot in mouth, draw tight slowly. Trim tag ends.

Nail Knot.

Lay hollow tube alongside fly line. Wrap 4 to 6 wraps of backing or leader butt forward over the tube and line. Run end of backing or leader through the tube.

Pinch knot with finger and thumb, slide it off tube, draw ends of backing or leader in opposite directions to seat knot firmly and neatly. Trim tag ends.

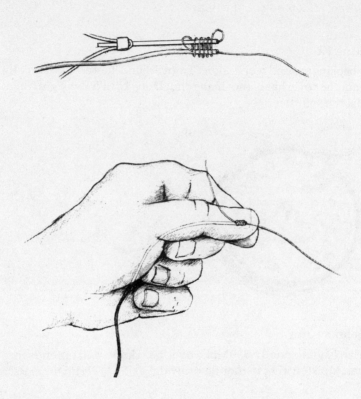

Blood Knot.

Overlap the two ends to be joined by 5″ to 6″. (Note: Use surgeon's knot if the two sections are of greatly different diameters.)

Wrap one end around opposite section five times. Run tag end through gap between sections. Pull tag out an inch or two.

Transfer knot to opposite hand. Wrap other tag end around opposite section five times, reversing direction of wraps. Run end through gap and pull tag out an inch or two. Moisten knot in mouth, draw it down slowly and firmly. Trim tag ends.

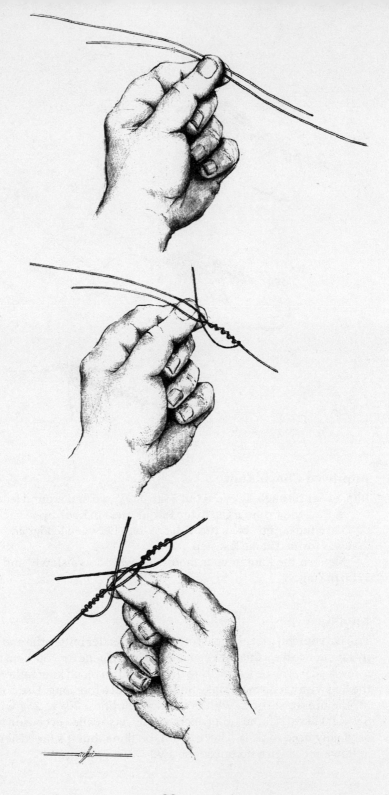

Improved Clinch Knot.

Run leader through fly eye about 3″ to 4″. Wrap end around leader five times. Run end through gap in the leader, next to hook eye.

Turn the tag end back through the loop between leader and tag end that was formed in the last step.

Moisten the knot in your mouth, draw it down slowly and firmly. Trim the tag.

Knot tip.

To save yourself a lot of knot tying, attach a leader butt to the end of your fly line, and leave it there permanently. Then whenever you want to tie on a new leader, you tie it directly to the butt with a blood knot rather than to the line with a nail knot. Make this butt about a foot long. Use 30# to 40# for the proper stiffness with 6- to 8-weight lines, 20# to 25# with 3- to 5-weight lines. (The nail knot, incidentally, is so called because a nail was originally used to tie it. That can still be done, but it's far easier with a hollow tube, even a streamside straw.)

FLY BOXES

Fly boxes are designed to store, protect, and prevent the disastrous spillage of the flies with which you'll fish. Different fly boxes serve different purposes; the same box that holds your dry flies will not be best for your nymphs and streamers. It's wise, before buying any boxes, to be sure that they're not too large to fit into the fastened pockets of your fishing vest.

Dry Fly Box.

Dry flies should be stored loose in a box with open compartments. This will keep the hackles from matting and otherwise bending the flies out of shape, so they refuse to float right. Don't crowd them. When you've settled on a few favorite patterns, tie them in a narrow range of sizes. Then store them in the dry fly box, each size and kind to its own compartment. The best boxes have lids you can see through, so that you can do some selecting before the lid is lifted.

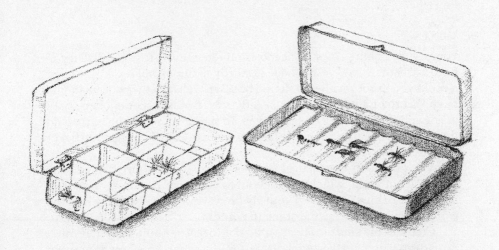

Wet Fly, Nymph, and Streamer Boxes.

Sunk flies have swept-back hackles, and can stand being stuck into foam and crowded in rows. It's preferable to store them in ridged boxes, because then it's easier to keep them sorted out, and to see when it's time to select one. If you use more than a few of each type, it's best to have a separate box for wets, nymphs, and streamers.

25

VESTS

For most fly fishing, a vest is the most convenient way to carry all that you need astream. A good vest is made of sturdy material, but not so thick that it cooks you in hot weather. It should be sewn well, and the pockets should have Velcro or zipper fastenings. A fly vest needs lots of pockets, both inside and out. The pockets should vary in size, from small enough to hold tippet spools and fly dressing, to large enough to hold the biggest fly boxes you intend to carry.

Vests come in two critical lengths: normal and short. Though the normal length vest, which hangs about to your belt, is satisfactory for 90 percent of fishing, it will dip your fly boxes and other gadgetry into the water if you wade deep (the other 10 percent).

Consider the kind of water you'll get into before buying a vest. If you'll be in deep water at all, get a short vest with as many pockets as you can find. That is this author's solution, since he's had to dry out too many fly boxes to keep hooks from rusting, and he's too lazy to transfer his equipage from vest to vest every time he fishes different kinds of water. He has one vest; it's a shorty.

THE WELL-STOCKED VEST

The well-stocked vest will contain some essentials that are critical to your angling enjoyment, and sometimes to your angling success. A basic list includes: *Leader nippers* on a pin-on spring retriever; *hemostat* with which to release fish; *hook hone* to sharpen hooks; *fly floatant* to dress your dries; *line cleaner* to use once a day whether you think you need to or not; *handkerchief* to dry your fly and wipe your hands; *tippet dispenser* or spare tippet spools; *sunglasses* and *sunscreen; toilet paper;* and small *flashlight*.

During a long day astream, you'll want to be able to add a lunch in the back cargo pocket of your vest, plus a flat bottle full of water, juice, or whatever you prefer.

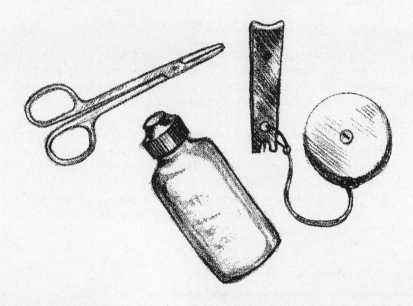

Alternatives to Vests.

The first alternative is simply a shirt with lots of pockets. If you're going to be fishing in a place that's difficult to reach, or going backpacking, or just desire to travel light, pare things down to the minimum. Carry them in a shirt or in a tiny purse-like creel that is the perfect alternative to a vest.

WADERS

The best waders are stocking-foot neoprenes, along with felt-soled wading brogues that have hard sides and steel shanks. Neoprenes keep you warm in cold water. They are buoyant, serving as life preservers should you take a tumble. Sturdy boots protect your feet from rock bruises, and give you sure footing.

Second best—perhaps best if you fish in water that's above 60 degrees most of the time—are lightweight stocking-foot waders made of coated nylon, also with sturdy wading shoes. These are cooler, not so bulky, not so heavy. But they do not float you.

An alternative is bootfoot waders in either neoprene or nylon: waders that have boots attached. They don't protect the feet quite so well, but they are far easier to get on and off.

Under the Waders.

Always wear waders over sweat pants, polypro long johns, or just shorts if the weather is hot. Jeans, khakis, and cords adhere to the inside of the waders, bind, and are fatiguing if you fish for longer than a brief time.

Traction.

Always wear felt-soled boots or shoes. They stick to clean stones, and save spills a dozen times a day. If you wade streams coated with silt or algae, then add studs, cleats, or chains. If you fish lots of different water types, then buy felt-soled boots, and carry slip-on cleats or chains for those waters where you need them.

WADING SAFETY

If the water you intend to wade has any depth and potential danger to it, be sure to carry a wading staff. Also cinch a belt around your waist to prevent your waders from filling entirely if you should take a plunge. Tie the staff to the belt with a couple of feet of cord.

When wading boisterous water, always keep one foot and the staff planted, and do not move the trailing foot until the leading foot has found a firm seat on the bottom. If the water is pushy, use the staff on the upstream side; lean into the current and onto the staff at the same time.

If you should ever get knocked loose from your moorings and fail to regain your footing, don't panic; you're just in for a wet ride. Let your feet ride up to the surface and keep them downstream ahead of you to fend off rocks. Backpaddle with your hands; remain calm until you get back into shallow water or can reach shore.

Chapter 3
Basic Fly Casting

Fly casting is a matter of causing the rod to bend and then recoil out its bend in such a way that it propels the line in the direction and distance that you desire. The rod responds much more to timing and grace than to strength. Let that be your guide as you begin learning to cast a fly: grace is your goal, and once you've achieved it, distance and accuracy will follow. If you try to apply power without grace, the results will be an elemental tangle.

Extending the distance you can cast, later, is a matter of learning how to apply more power—more rod speed and therefore more line speed—smoothly and at the right time. In other words, you extend the cast by learning perfect grace on a short cast, then slowly extending the distance you can handle gracefully.

Before stringing your rod and starting to cast on a lawn or at the edge of a pond or lake, take time to pace off 20', 30', 40', and 60'. Impress on yourself how near 20' is to you, how far 60' is away. Many fish are caught at 20', an easy cast; most fish are caught at less than 40', which you will master quickly and with ease; few fish are caught at 60', a long cast even for an expert. Your goal, here at the start, is a graceful 25' to 35' cast.

WHERE AND WHEN TO PRACTICE

It's best to hold your initial practice sessions on mowed grass, with lots of room around you. Your own back lawn is great; a city park works well, especially if you can find a corner where you will not be disturbed. A paved parking lot is an alternative to grass, but it will destroy a fly line, so be prepared to learn on one, then buy another when you go fishing.

The edge of a lake will work for much of your practice, but be sure you are there to learn to cast, not to catch fish. The worst place to learn to fly fish is out on a stream, where you're tempted to try for fish at the same moment that you're trying to learn the movements that make a fly cast.

When to Practice.

You'll be surprised how few sessions it will take on a lawn before you're ready to head out to a stream and get attached to a fish. But discipline yourself to at least four or five sessions, over a period of a week or two. Keep the sessions short: do not practice until your wrist and arm become tired and sore. Instead, quit and come back the next day. An hour or so makes a practical limit at first, and you'll stop while you're still fresh and eager, which will draw you back for more later.

Stringing the Rod.

Join the sections of the rod together firmly, with the guides aligned. Attach the reel, then double the line near its tip, and push this doubled end through the guides. Tie on a leader, and a fly with the barb cut off, or a small piece of yarn.

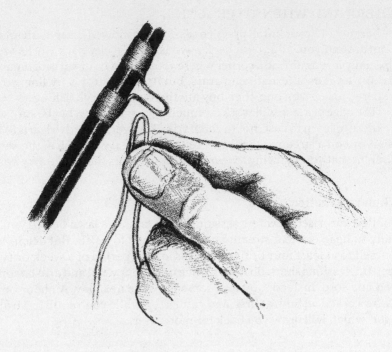

PREPARATION FOR THE CAST

Getting Line Out.

As a practicality, you need to begin your first cast with about 25′ to 30′ of line out in front of you. Since you have not yet learned how to cast it out there, strip line off your reel, lay down your rod, and walk the line out there. This is a reason not to make your first session on water.

A Hint About Practice.

Learning the motions that make the basic casting stroke is the key to graceful fly casting. You can practice all the steps in the basic stroke right in your easy chair. Just remove the tip section from your rod, take the right grip on the rod handle, and push it slowly through the proper motions. This trains the wrist and arm to memorize the parts of the stroke in the correct sequence.

The Grip.

The best grip on the fly rod handle is a rather loose one. Wrap the four fingers of your rod hand, whether it's the right or the left, around the cork, and align your thumb on top of it. Your thumb serves to aim the rod, and therefore the cast. It also serves to stop the rod on the backcast, which, as you will see in the following pages, is very important.

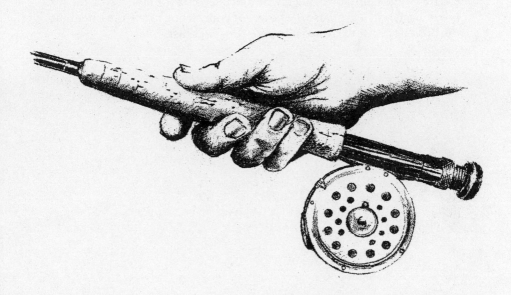

THE BASIC BACKCAST

Begin the basic backcast with 25' to 30' of line out on the lawn. Hold the rod straight out in front of you and pointed down the line. With a smooth and rapid movement, lift the rod to a 45-degree angle, picking up the back of the line and setting it in motion toward you. Do not jerk the rod and make the line jump; do not dally with the rod and let the line settle toward the ground. Lift it smoothly to *load* the rod for the power stroke.

Without hesitation, make the *power stroke* by accelerating the rod swiftly from the 45-degree position in front of you to an 80-degree position just behind you, but still almost straight overhead. Stop it there abruptly. Two things will help you in this. First, the thumb on the grip will restrict rod travel and help stop it quickly. Second, keeping your wrist straight, not breaking it, will let you use the power of your strong forearm rather than the power of your weak wrist to make the backcast.

The proper *stop*, illustrated here, is just as important as the proper loading and powering of the rod. If you stop too soon, with the rod too high, the line will be thrown almost straight overhead behind you. If you stop too late, with the rod too low, the line will be driven into the ground or brush behind you. This is the most common mistake in all of fly casting: dropping the rod on the backcast. Position your feet so that you are able to watch the backcast over your shoulder. Work on it until it travels level, or slightly higher than level.

An effective forecast can begin only after the line has straightened out in the air behind you. While the line straightens, let the rod drift back beyond the 80-degree position at which you stopped it, to 45 degrees. This drift will put you in position to load the rod on the forecast. (Remember that you can practice these basic moves using just the butt of the rod, while you read the book, sitting in your chair at home.)

THE BASIC FORECAST

You *load* the rod on the forecast by moving it briskly but smoothly forward from 45 degrees to about the 60-degree position behind your shoulder. Watch the line, and begin this movement only when it is straight, or nearly so. Move the rod forward with your forearm, do not break your wrist, and do not jerk.

This loading of the rod flows without pause into the next step, the power stroke.

Now rapidly accelerate the rod from 60 degrees behind you to 80 degrees ahead, just past straight overhead. Use a driving movement of the forearm and wrist. The most common mistake is to hold the forearm rigid and use just the wrist. Instead, use the same stroke with which you'd drive a big nail. Use the force of your arm; don't merely tap at the rod with your wrist.

Wrist casting won't give you either grace or line speed; all you'll get is a sore wrist after an hour or so of fishing.

Stop the rod abruptly at the 80-degree point. This stop allows the rod to spring powerfully out of the deep bend you've put into it. High line speed comes from the stop as much as it does from the start. Don't swish the rod lazily back and forth.

Again, the stop must be timed right: too soon and the line flies high, too late and the line drives into the ground. When the forecast is perfect, it will sail out level with the ground or at an angle slightly upward.

While the line follows the rod tip and straightens out in front of you, let the rod drift slightly forward to the 45-degree position. This will put you in position to load the rod for the next backcast.

However, on the first few practice casts, it's best to let the forecast straighten out in the air in front of you, then let it drop to the ground. Begin from there, working on a single backcast and forecast until you've got the four parts of the rod movement down: *load, power, stop,* and *drift.*

THE BASIC FORECAST AND BACKCAST

Once you've mastered both the single forecast and backcast, then it's time to begin carrying them in the air: weaving a series of forecasts and backcasts. All you've got to do differently is to watch your forecast loop unfurl in front of you. Once it is straight, begin another backcast rather than letting it drop to the ground.

Any problems you have in your casting stroke will become magnified and multiplied as you carry a series of fore- and backcasts in the air. If you begin to get tangled, or start to get slack in the line, drop the cast and start again.

The basic casting plane should be level with the ground, front and back. Imagine yourself casting alongside a house—the line should loop back and forth parallel to the eaves. If it doesn't, work on the arc of the rod until it does.

If your line drives toward the ground on fore- and backcasts—the most common mistake—practice starting the power on your rod at the 60-degree front and back positions. Then make your stops abruptly just beyond straight overhead. The narrowness of that casting arc, and the speed with which you move your rod within it, are the keys to successful casting.

LOOP CONTROL

A tight loop is the key to distance casting: the less air the front end of the line has to cut, the farther you'll be able to cast. To achieve a tight loop, shorten up the *power stroke*. Make the rod tip move a shorter distance, but faster, by making the power and the stop abrupt, like a hammer stroke.

The major function of the open loop is to reduce tangles when you cast split shot, strike indicators, and nymphs all on the same leader. An open loop is also useful for casting large flies, or heavily weighted flies. To achieve an open loop, simply move the rod through a longer and slower arc during the power stroke. The casting plane should still be parallel to those imaginary eaves of a house.

Note on Loop Control.

When practicing loop control, be sure to look over your shoulder, so you can watch the change as you lengthen and shorten your power stroke, thus opening and closing the width of the line loop in the air.

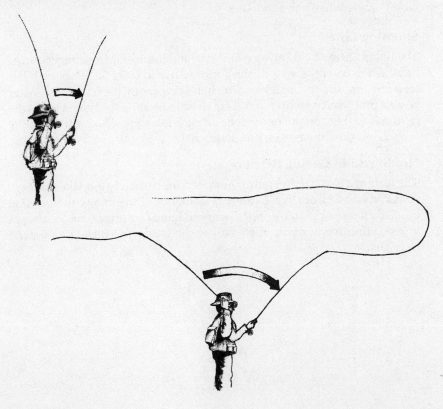

FUNCTIONS OF THE LINE HAND

Holding Loose Line.

The line hand is used to gather and hold loops of retrieved line. This is important on long casts, especially when you're wading deep. Each loop should hold about 4' to 8' of line. If you hold more than one loop, each successive loop should be a bit shorter than the one before it, so that they won't tangle when you shoot line.

Shooting Line.

The line is always held between the line hand thumb and forefinger during a cast. Casts usually start with the line drawn in to 25' or 30'. To extend line, let a few feet slip through your line hand fingers on each forecast. After you've practiced it awhile, you'll get used to holding the line in loops the right size so that you can release one on each forecast, when you're casting long. Loops are unnecessary on short casts.

Holding Line During Retrieve.

The instant a cast is delivered to the water, immediately loop the line over your rod hand forefinger. Draw any slack out of the line with your line hand. By keeping all slack *behind* your rod hand forefinger, you're always in a position to vary your retrieve, set the hook, or lift the line for the next cast.

DELIVERY STROKE

The delivery stroke is the last forecast that lays the fly out exactly where you want it on the water. After you've put the power into the cast, let the rod drift down until it is level with the water.

When you're fishing a dry fly and want your line, leader, and fly to settle gently so they don't frighten fish, aim your delivery stroke about waist high above the water. Then the line straightens out first, and the fly settles lightly to the water second. If you aim right at the water, the line and fly will smack into it.

If you're casting a long distance, especially if you want to shoot some extra line into the cast, aim the delivery stroke head high or even higher. This simply buys time from gravity while the last loop unfurls and the line shoots out, before the line is pulled down to the water.

Shooting Line.

When casting 50' or more, don't try to carry all that line in the air on each forecast and backcast. Instead, carry about 40' and hold the extra line in coils in your line hand. On the delivery stroke, simply let go of those coils after you've completed the power stroke, and the line in the air will pull the line in the coils right out behind it.

TAILING LOOP

You'll have to deal with tailing loops often in your first few days of casting practice. Later, they'll crop up on occasion and frustrate you astream. They occur when the upper part of the line loop rides down below the lower part of the loop, and the two parts of the loop cross and tangle in the air. The tailing loop is almost always caused by getting the *power stroke* ahead of the *loading movement*.

To cure tailing loops, practice the casting stroke with just the butt section of your rod: load, power, stop, and drift on the backcast and on the forecast. Repeat these movements with your rod butt, or even just your hand. Then try casting again, and it's likely your tailing loops will be gone.

CHANGING DIRECTIONS OF THE CAST

You'll often want to lift your line off the water from one direction and lay out the next cast in another. The line always follows the direction the rod tip travels. Just pick up the line as you normally would, then angle the rod toward the new direction on each subsequent forecast and backcast until you've got the line aimed where you want it.

SIDEARM CAST

To make a sidearm cast, simply tilt the rod over until it's parallel with the water. When casting, all of the earlier principles apply; load, power, stop, and let the backcast drift, then load, power, stop, and let the forecast straighten in front of you. Because gravity tugs the line toward the water, you won't be able to cast great distances with the sidearm cast.

Uses of the Sidearm Cast.

The most obvious use is to snake your line beneath overhanging branches, in order to poke your fly to fish holding in those lies that other folks rarely reach.

It also helps to tilt your rod into the sidearm cast any time you approach so closely to trout that you can see them. Your rod waving high in the air is very visible to them, and will frighten them. Tip it over to cast and they won't see it.

THE SINGLE HAUL

When you're ready to begin casting for distance, say 55′ to 60′ and beyond, the first strategy is to tighten up your loops by shortening the power stroke. Once you've got that down, then it's time to increase your line speed. You've already done part of that by achieving a narrow loop. You can add to it by speeding up the power stroke—once you've learned to do so gracefully. You can never gain distance at the expense of grace.

The *single haul* is another way to increase line speed dramatically. It will increase the load on the rod during the critical power stroke. This increased load cocks the spring that is the rod down deeper, causing it to go off with more power when it punches out the forecast.

To execute the single haul, let your line hand trail up near the reel while the rod drifts on the backcast. Now bring the rod forward to load it for the forward cast. Just as you turn it over into the power stroke, draw your line hand down swiftly. The power stroke and the haul are simultaneous movements, and quite abrupt, so the proper timing will take some practice.

THE DOUBLE HAUL

The double haul is simply a single haul extended to both forecast and backcast. It is the ultimate way to increase your line speed, and therefore the distance you can cast.

Start the double haul with your line hand near the reel as you begin the backcast. At the power stroke, simultaneously draw the line hand downward sharply. While the line straightens and the rod drifts back, lift your line hand up to the reel again.

Load the rod for the forecast, then draw your line hand down swiftly at the same time that you tip the rod over in the power stroke. Lift your line hand to the reel again as the forecast loop rolls out. This puts you in position to make the haul on the backcast, to repeat the double haul cycle.

Note on the Double Haul.

Two cycles of backcast and forecast will extract all you can get out of the double haul. Never hold the line in the air for several cycles; it's a waste of energy, and keeps your fly out of the water.

ROLL CAST

You'll often get into situations in which brush or a steep bank stand right behind you, and you can't make a normal backcast. You can still roll cast 25' to 45' of line.

Begin the roll cast by shaking line past the rod tip, and letting it lie on the water. Draw the rod back to a position about 1 o'clock behind your right shoulder. Now wait a moment while the line follows and drops into a curve behind the rod.

Complete the roll cast by driving the rod forward in a normal power stroke. It should be short and fast, and stop with the rod in the normal 80-degree position, to form a loop of line traveling out over the water. Do not drive the rod all the way forward or no loop will form. However, after you've started the loop rolling, let the rod follow it as you would with a delivery stroke, so that the rod ends level with the water.

TILTING THE CASTING PLANE

The normal casting plane is level with the ground as you practice, parallel to the water when you step into it or paddle onto it later to go fishing.

If you've got tall grass or low brush behind you, and want to lift your backcast over it, then you're defeated unless you can tilt the casting plane, lifting the backcast high behind you. This is such a common problem that learning to tilt the casting plane is critical to your fishing success. Incorporate it into your practice once you've mastered the normal plane.

The casting plane is tilted by tipping the arc of the power stroke slightly forward. Picture the face of a clock. If the normal power stroke covers the distance between 11 and 2, to tilt the plane up in back, make the power stroke between 12 and 2. To tilt the plane down in back—a rare need indeed—power the cast between 10 and 12 on the clock face, and you'll have a low backcast and high forecast.

MENDING LINE

Many times when you're fishing across a current, it will push a *downstream belly* into your line. The fatter line behind the thin front taper catches more current, and trots downstream faster than the tip. The line forms a belly, and this tugs at the fly and causes it to race. If you're fishing a dry, you've got drag. More often, it happens when you're fishing a wet fly or streamer, which then races faster than any natural food form might swim. No fish will take it. You've got to slow it down.

Use upstream mends to take the belly out of the line, and slow the drift or swing of the fly. To do this, point the rod tip down the line, then lift the rod outward and upward with vigor, and roll it over upstream. The line lifts with the rod, arcs over, and lands on the water again in an *upstream belly*. It's often necessary to repeat the mend several times on a single cast to continue the proper drift or swing.

If you're fishing slow water with wet flies or streamers, and want to speed the drift, you can use downstream mends to install a downstream belly in the line, and speed the fly.

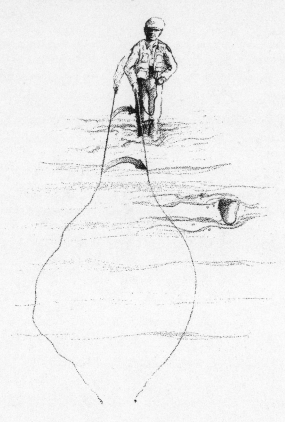

Chapter 4
Hooking and Playing Fish

The best way to set the hook varies with the size hook you're using, the stiffness of the rod, and the hardness of the mouth of the fish you are trying to set the hook into.

Large Dry Flies.
Takes to these can be quick. Set the hook as soon as you see the take, raising the rod sharply and swiftly.

Small Dry Flies.
Takes to small dries are normally slow and deliberate, and you'll be fishing fine tippets. Set the hook by lifting the rod firmly but not abruptly.

Atlantic Salmon, Steelhead, and Wet Flies.
If you feel a tap and jerk the rod, you'll pull the fly away from the fish or break it off. It's best to do nothing and let the fish hook itself.

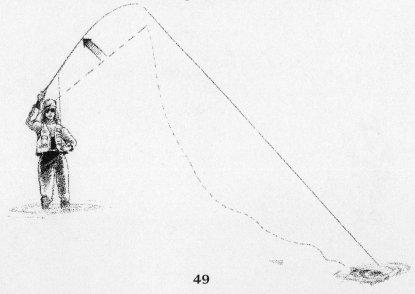

Streamers and Saltwater Flies.

Fish usually take streamers with such thuds that they hook themselves. But if you're fishing for species with hard mouths, rap the hook home hard.

Poppers and Hair Bugs.

You've usually got to jab the hook into the hard jaw of a bass. Lift the rod and hit the fish sharply.

PLAYING FISH

Small fish can be played by hand, stripping line over the forefinger of your rod hand to lead them in. But larger fish should be played off the reel. Reel slack out of the line and put the pull directly against the drag as quickly as you can.

The flex in the rod, combined with the drag of the reel, saps the strength of a big fish. To let the rod do its work, hold it high, so that it bends in a grand arc toward the fish. This bend serves to tire the fish, and also is the perfect shock absorber to protect your tippet. But if the fish is powerful, then hold the rod lower so the strength of the fish is pitted against the strong butt of the rod.

Never let slack get into your line between you and the fish. It will allow the fish to slip the hook, or you'll get the line tangled, or the fish will make a surge the other way at the instant you get the slack out and pull your way: snap!

When a fish jumps, lower your rod toward it quickly. You don't want the fish to land on a tight tippet. It can break off, or the hook can pull out.

LANDING FISH

Hand-Landing Fish.

It's often convenient to fish without carrying a net. But you've then got to land your fish by hand. This can be difficult if you don't play them until they're tired. You should be able to lead a fish to your hand while it's lying on its side. Hold your hand in position just under the water, and slide the fish over it. Lift gently from beneath the fish, cradling it. Do not squeeze. If the fish thrashes, don't try to chase it down. Play it out and try again.

Netting Fish.

It's always easier to net a fish, and can also be better for the fish if you intend to release it, because there's no need to exhaust it. Use a net with cotton mesh, not nylon, which scrapes the fish. The secret to successful netting is to place the net half in and half out of water, then lead the fish into it headfirst. Never stab the net at a fish, or try to catch it from behind. And never try to land one while it's still green, fighting hard.

RELEASING FISH

Releasing fish is a way to ensure good fishing for the future. Unhook a fish as quickly as possible. Carry and use a hemostat. If the hook is buried deep, just break it off. The fish will get rid of it later. Don't lift any fish out of water for more than 30 to 45 seconds; a fish has little blood, runs out of oxygen far faster than you do, and will die later.

Always revive a fish before releasing it. Cradle it in the water with one hand and restrain it by the wrist of the tail with the other. Hold it until it has recovered its strength; don't let go until the fish swims strongly out of your hands.

De-Barbing Your Hook.

Pinching the barb on your hook makes it a lot easier to set into a fish, so you'll catch more fish, not fewer. It also makes the fish far easier to release.

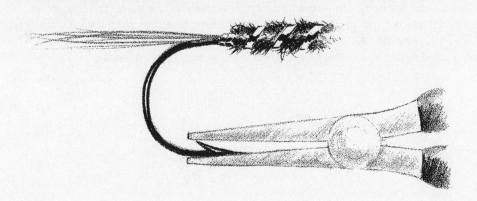

Chapter 5
Fly Fishing for Trout in Streams

The pursuit of trout in running water has long been the mainstream of fly fishing. New feeder streams have opened out, some just lately: trout in lakes, bass and panfish, salmon and steelhead, the vast horizons of saltwater. But flowing streams harboring trout remain the main water in which we wade.

Fly fishing for trout in streams has more facets than almost any other branch of the sport. You'll want to slowly master casting, then learn something about trout: their senses and their needs, how to read water and find them, what foods they eat, and how to choose flies that will fool them.

It's a subject that will continue to challenge you forever. At the same time, it's a sport that will reward you almost instantly. Once you've learned to cast 20' to 30', you're going to go out and start catching a few trout right away.

THE SPECIES OF TROUT

The *rainbow trout* is the species most likely to be caught today, around the country and even around the world. It is a hardy fish, and adapts to a wide variety of trout stream conditions. It was originally a West Coast species; its sea-going form is the steelhead. Its favorite waters are swift and cold, with lots of rapids and riffles. The rainbow is recognized by the reddish stripe, sometimes faint, along its sides.

The *brook trout* is a native of the East, from Hudson's Bay south to the mountains of Georgia. It is truly a char, not a trout. Its range is restricted to clean waters with lots of oxygen. Its native habitat has fallen to logging and industry; its range is not as widespread as it once was. But it has been successfully planted in the West and in South America. The brookie can be identified by the vermiculated patterning on its back.

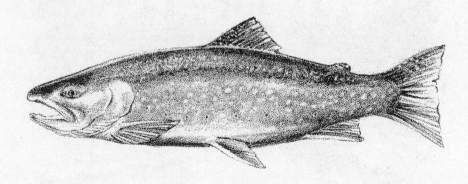

The *brown trout* was imported to North America from Germany and Scotland in two separate transplants. It has adapted here to slightly warmer and less clean waters that brook trout were no longer able to survive. But browns do well in pristine waters, in both the East and West. They can be recognized by their black spots surrounded by faint red halos.

The *cutthroat trout* is native to the West, like the rainbow, but it has not enjoyed the widespread transport given that hardier, more aggressive species. The cutt doesn't do so well in hatcheries, and is still found most commonly in its native range along the Pacific coast and on the spine of the Rockies in the Yellowstone and Snake River regions. The cutthroat can be recognized by the crimson gill slashes on the undersides of its jaws.

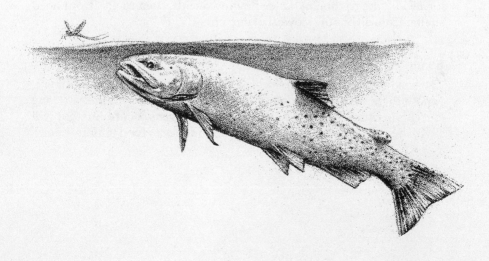

THE NEEDS OF TROUT

Trout have a few simple needs, and they'll be found only in water that meets them. Within a stream or lake, they'll be happiest where these needs are provided for in abundance. Find water that meets their needs, and that's where you'll find the trout.

Temperature and Oxygen.

Trout are most active in water in a temperate range from 45 to 65 degrees. They'll be sluggish in water below 40 degrees and begin to be stressed at around 70 degrees. Most trout perish when the water reaches 80 degrees. In water that hot, they become starved for oxygen; it's hard to tell if heat or lack of oxygen kills them.

Protection from Predators.

Trout need defense against predators such as birds, otters, and anglers. They find protection from birds overhead through their camouflaged coloration, and also by seeking the shelter of depth. For protection from otters, they depend on warning vibrations striking their lateral line. Their primary line of defense against us is their fine-tuned sight.

Shelter from Current.

Trout quickly become exhausted if they are forced to swim against a current. They have little stamina. That is why they are found in the soft spots above and below boulders, and in the slow water along the bottom formed by the friction of water flowing over bottom rocks. Trout need shelter from all but the slowest of currents.

Food.

The need to feed often overrides all other needs. That is why trout will expose themselves to predators on flats, or swim out to brave strong currents in riffles, whenever a heavy hatch of insects occurs. But they will slight their other needs only when an abundance of food tempts them.

TROUT SIGHT

Because of the wavelike nature of light, most rays hitting the water at the lowest angles glance off the surface like skipped stones. As a consequence, a trout is unable to see anything that lies beneath a 10-degree line of sight onto the outside world. At 10' from the trout, you've got to be on your belly, and keep your rod tipped over to the side, to be out of sight. At 20' you can fish while kneeling and still stay out of sight. At 30' you can stoop, or wade just a couple of feet deep. At 40' you can stand up to fish, and the trout will not be able to see you.

Because of the way all light rays are bent when they enter water, trout see all objects above their low line of sight as objects looming around the edge of a circular window onto the outside world. If you're 30' to 40' away, you'll be a dim outline at the edge of this circle. Move slowly, dress drably, and they'll likely not notice you.

OTHER TROUT SENSES

Smell.

We don't smell like roses to trout, and they have an excellent sense of smell. That's why it's wise to wear waders even when you're fishing water warm enough so that you don't need them. They contain your evil scent. Be sure to keep such violent scents as mosquito repellant and sunscreen lotion away from your flies, your line, and your leader. Trout take dry flies by sight, so floatants don't prohibit hits. But if you get any strong odor on a wet, streamer, or nymph, you won't get into many dances with trout.

Taste.

Flies aren't going to be tasty to trout, no matter what you do to improve them. That's why they take them in and spit them back out so quickly. But you can do something about the tactile sense: the way a fly feels to the trout once it's taken into the mouth. If the fly is hard, for example, wound with a body of monofilament, it will be rejected quickly. If it is soft, say, made of dubbed fur, the fish might hold onto it long enough for you to get the hook set.

Hearing.

Little in the way of sound transfers from the air to the water, so you are free to shout and laugh. Trout will never hear you. But they are very sensitive to any sounds made in or under the water. Bang the side of your boat, they are gone. Wade recklessly, knocking rocks together, and you'll never wade near enough to catch them.

Lateral Line.

The lateral line of all fish is a sense organ, in a way an extension of the sense of hearing. It picks up low-level vibrations, and gives you more reason to avoid making noise in your boat or while wading. The lateral line also senses changes in temperature, so that trout can seek waters most congenial to them.

TROUT FOOD FORMS AND THE WAY FLIES IMITATE THEM

Mayfly adult
Mayfly nymph
Caddisfly adult
Caddisfly pupa
Caddisfly larva
Stonefly adult
Stonefly nymph
Sculpin
Minnow

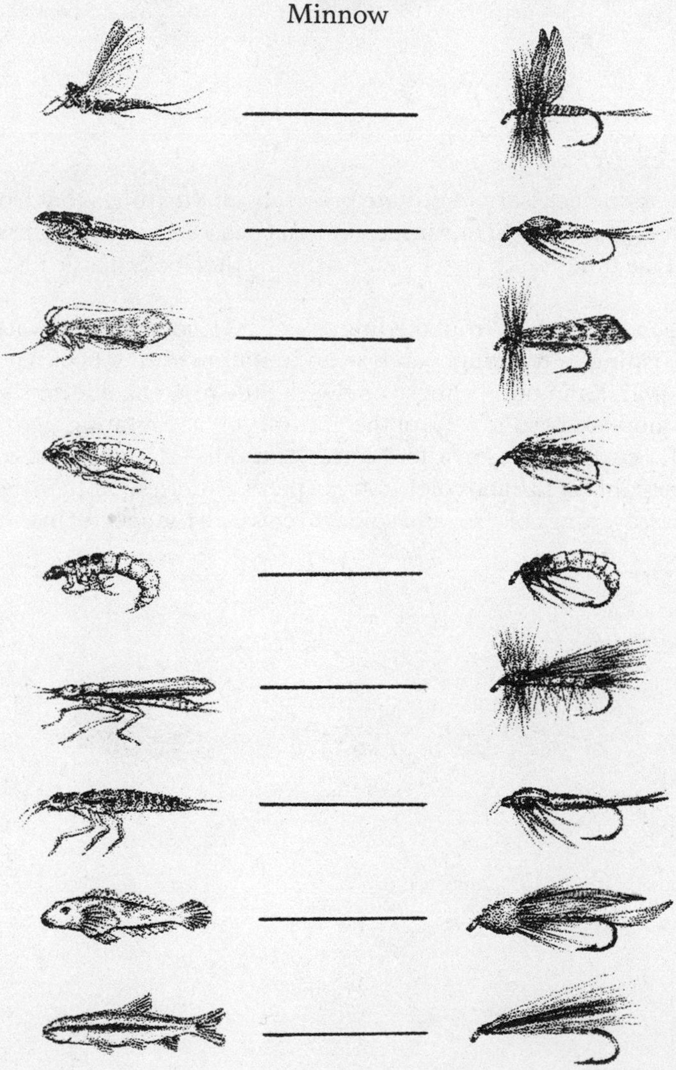

_____

_____

_____

_____

_____

_____

_____

_____

_____

DRY FLY TYPES

It's not often necessary to imitate precisely all the things that trout eat. They rarely feed on just one insect, but take whatever nature offers them. Most of the time you can get by with a dry fly that looks a little like a lot of insects.

When you do find trout feeding selectively, consider the water type you're fishing. If it's rough, choose an imitation with lots of hackle for flotation. If it's smooth, choose one with little or no hackle, to show the trout a more exact silhouette of the natural you're imitating.

All species within an order—here the caddis—have the same shape. They vary only in size and color. You can pick a pattern style, then tie or buy it in a narrow range of sizes and colors to cover all the species in the order.

AN EFFECTIVE DRY FLY BOX

Adams (#12-#18), Blue-wing Olive (#12-#16), Light Cahill (#12-#16)

Adams Parachute (#12-#16), Olive Thorax (#12-#16), Grizzly Wulff (#10-#14)

Royal Wulff (#8-#14), Humpy (#8-#14), Royal Trude (#8-#12)

Olive Sparkle Dun (#16-#20), March Brown Comparadun (#12-#16), Pale Morning Natural Dun (#16-#18)

Stimulator (#6-#12), Sofa Pillow (#6-#12)

Elk Hair Caddis (#12-#16), Kings River Caddis (#12-#16), Bucktail Caddis (#12-#16)

Joe's Hopper (#8-#12), Letort Hopper (#8-#14)

DRY FLY TECHNIQUES

The goal when fishing a dry fly is to show it to the fish as if it were a natural insect adrift on the water, not attached to a line or a leader.

Tackle.

The line must float; clean and dress it. The leader should be 8' long for rough water, 12' long for smooth. Make sure your tippet is at least 2' long; 3' to 4' is better for the glassy currents of flats. The tippet must be the right diameter for the fly. (See chart page 19)

Delicacy.

The fly should land softly on the water. Aim your delivery stroke about 3' above the surface; this allows the line and leader to straighten in the air, the fly to descend gently, and the leader tippet to recoil slightly. This slack in the leader lets the fly drift freely, as if unattached. If the leader lands exactly straight, it will soon catch the currents and tug the fly around. You'll never notice it, but the trout will. They'll refuse the fly.

Control of the Cast.

The closer you approach to trout, or to a suspected lie, the better control you'll have over your cast and over the drift of the fly. Get into the habit of making most of your dry fly casts at around 25' to 40', kneeling or stooping where you must to stay below the line of sight of the trout.

DRAG-FREE DRIFT

Drag.

Your worst enemy, when dry fly fishing, is drag: the leader getting straight and towing the fly in an unnatural manner. Sometimes it leaves a wake. More often the movement is too slight for you to notice at casting distance.

Conflicting Currents.

The most common cause of drag is surface currents that run in more than one direction. Sometimes there's just a couple of them, one tugging your leader west while the other tugs the fly east. At other times there's a seething of currents; the leader and fly are torn in many different directions; slack goes out of the tippet; and drag sets in.

Position.

There is almost always one direction that is the best approach to rising trout, or to the expected lie of a trout. Try to put all conflicting currents behind you. If the currents are of a single *sheet* of speed between you and the drift lane of the fly, the dry will float at the same speed as the line and leader, and you'll get a drag-free drift. Before you ever make a cast, get into the habit of scanning the water and looking for the single best place to position yourself for the cast. Wade cautiously to that precise position.

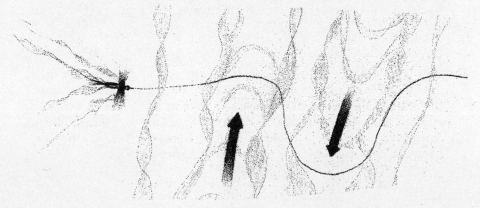

FISHING THE SEARCHING DRY FLY

Most of the time when you're fishing dry flies for trout, you'll see sporadic rises, perhaps no rises at all. You won't be able to pinpoint fish and cast to them. You'll want to *search the water,* fishing all likely spots you think might hold trout.

Water Types.

Don't search water that's so fast trout couldn't swim against it. They won't be there. Don't fish water so deep that trout wouldn't bother going all the way up for a dry. The searching dry works best in riffles and runs that are 2' to 5' deep, with modest to brisk currents. The method is at its best where the water is rumpled on top, reflecting a bouldery bottom. If a few boulders break the surface, that's better water.

Covering the Water.

Fish the searching dry with upstream casts, 20' to 40' long. Set up a disciplined casting pattern that covers all of the water with short casts. Cover what you can from one position, then move upstream to a new position, and cover what you can from there. Be sure to cast carefully to any breaks in the current: boulders or logs or trenches. These are the most likely places to produce trout to the searching dry fly.

THE DRY FLY CAST QUARTERING UPSTREAM

Whenever you cast straight upstream, it tosses your line and leader right over the heads of the trout you're trying to catch. The fly alights, then drifts back down the same lane the line flew over on the way up. Trout are extremely wary about anything in the air above them, since they're so subject to predation from overhead. The flash of your line can send them fleeing. If it doesn't, the sight of your line and leader on the water, arriving ahead of the fly, can cause them to refuse it.

You can get away with a cast straight upstream in rough water. Anywhere else, it'll kill you. Avoid it. Wade into position so that you can cast quartering upstream and across, at a 30- to 60-degree angle. Do this whether you're fishing to visible rising trout, or to water that you suspect holds trout.

When the cast quarters across the current, the line never flies over the fish, and the fly drifts out at the end of the leader, to the surprise of the fish. They'll take it. Always make the first cast close, and place each subsequent cast a foot or two farther out. That way you constantly show the fly to trout that haven't seen your line or leader.

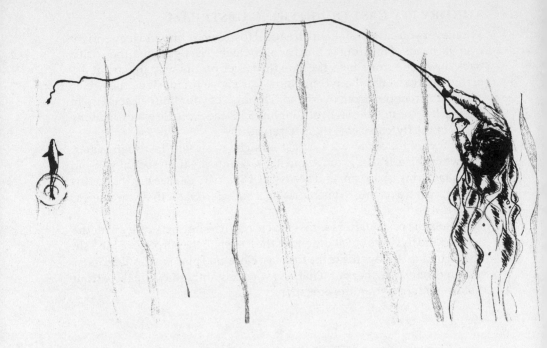

THE REACH CAST

Often you'll need to fish straight across the stream to rising trout, or to lies that you suspect hold trout. It's difficult to get a drag-free drift when casting across currents, especially if they are different speeds, which they usually are. But even if they aren't, the current will belly the line, and you've got almost instant drag.

To defeat this, use the reach cast when fishing cross-stream. It's easy. Just make a normal cast, aiming the delivery stroke where you want the fly to land. But while the line loop is still unfurling in the air, tip the rod far over in the upstream direction, then reach out with your arm. The fly will land where you aimed it, but the line will follow the rod tip, and land on the water at an angle across the currents between the fly and the rod tip, several feet upstream from the fly.

As the fly begins its float, simply follow it with your rod. When the fly passes straight in front of you, continue to follow and reach downstream with the rod, in order to extend the free drift of the fly. You can get a drift of 10′ to 20′ with the reach cast where a straight cast would give you just 1′ to 2′.

THE WIGGLE CAST

Rising trout feeding in smooth water will often be put off by any sign of the line and leader. The cast quartering upstream, and even the reach cast, can fail to fool them. The answer is the downstream wiggle cast, because it presents the fly floating *ahead* of the line and leader.

The problem, casting downstream, is to get a drag-free drift. Cast straight downstream and drag is instant. Instead, wade into position to cast quartering 30 to 60 degrees down to the fish. To introduce slack into the cast, make a normal cast, then wobble your rod tip side-to-side while the line is still in the air. The line and leader land on the water in S-curves. While these curves feed out, the fly floats freely downstream.

You'll be surprised how often the downstream wiggle cast fools trout that you thought refused you because your fly was the wrong one.

REFUSALS TO THE DRY FLY

Often trout rise to your dry fly and seem to take it, but you miss the strike. You'll think it's because you're too slow setting the hook.

More often, a missed strike is caused by the fish refusing your fly, rather than your failure to set the hook. The trout changes its mind at the last second; you see a boil, or a splash, but it's not a real take.

Leader Problems.

When you get refusals, check your leader first. Is it long enough? Is your tippet long and fine enough for the size fly you're fishing? If not, correct it.

Presentation.

Next, check your presentation. Are you getting drag you can't see? Is your leader arriving ahead of the fly, so trout see it and turn away? Move to the best casting position, and choose the best cast to avoid drag.

Fly Pattern.

The last thing to look at is the fly, which is the first thing most of us want to change. It's almost always best to go a size or two smaller, and a shade or two drabber, when you get refusals to a dry fly and need to change it.

DRY FLY TIPS

Fly Selection.

Develop a small list of dries with which you've had success, and that give you confidence. Keep them handy in a single fly box. They need not imitate particular insects, but should resemble in a broad way the natural foods that trout eat. The best dries resemble lots of different foods. The Adams, Elk Hair Caddis, Stimulator, and Humpy are examples.

Imitation.

When trout feed during a hatch of a single insect, you might need to match it to catch any fish. Capture a natural, and select the nearest thing in your fly box to it. If nothing works, consult with a fly shop later, or search for the insect in books. Find a fly or two for trial the next time you encounter the same insect. Over the years, you'll develop a short list of hatch-matching flies that work when trout are selective.

Presentation.

There is a long-standing argument between two schools of dry fly folks. One says imitation is most important. The other says presentation is most important. The truth is that both are important, but the best imitation will rarely take a fish if the presentation is poor. It's best to get both right.

Flotation.

If your dry fly fails to float, it won't fetch many fish. To keep it floating, use a handkerchief to dry the fly often, and then redress it with floatant. Watch an expert sometime. He constantly dresses his fly between pools, or between fish. He watches the water while he does it. This keeps his fly floating primly, but also causes him to slow down and assess the situation, so he is more apt to present the right fly in the right way, and therefore catch the right fish.

INTRODUCTION TO NYMPH FISHING

It has been said that trout do 80 to 90 percent of their feeding on the bottom, and that we merely skim the top of our opportunities when we restrict our fishing to dry flies. In large part this is true, although it's no reason to neglect the dry fly. But a person who learns nymphing more than doubles his opportunities to take trout.

When trout feed along the bottom, they take the immature stages of mayflies, stoneflies, caddisflies, midges, and a variety of less prolific organisms. It's a profusion that keeps trout pretty busy and very happy down there.

Aquatic insect populations manifest themselves up top only when it's time to hatch. Their presence is constant along the bottom, so trout feed on them at all times. Fish are always vulnerable to a nymph tumbled along the bottom. Most often trout accept whatever the current brings to them, which amounts to a smorgasbord. So, your nymph dressing doesn't need to be imitative; the best nymphs suggest many life forms.

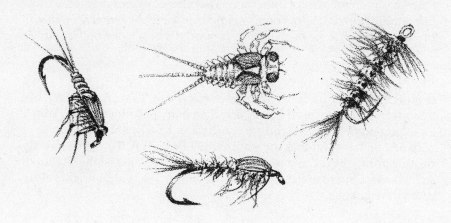

AN EFFECTIVE NYMPH BOX

Gold Ribbed Hare's Ear (#10-#16), Muskrat (#8-#14), Herl Nymph (#10-#14)

Pheasant Tail (#14-#18), Brassie (#12-#14), Zug Bug (#10-#14)

Kaufman's Stone (#4-#8), Bitch Creek (#4-#8)
Box Canyon Stone (#6-#10), Montana Stone (#4-#10)

Green Caddis Larva (#10-#14), Green Damsel (#10-#12), Olive Scud (#10-#14)

Tellico (#14-#18), Prince Nymph (#10-#14), TDC (#12-#14)

SPLIT SHOT AND INDICATOR TECHNIQUE

Since most natural nymphs eaten by trout are taken right along the bottom, it becomes important to master a method for getting your nymph imitation down to the same depth. The most effective way to do that is with the *split shot and strike indicator technique.* The method calls for the same floating line you've been using while fishing the dry fly.

The setup calls for a nymph at the end of a short tippet: 8″ to 10″. The tippet knot serves as a stop for one to four very small split shot: size BB or smaller. The leader should be 8′ to 10′ long. A foot or two from the end of the line, fix a bright strike indicator on the leader. This can be a cork ball with a hole drilled through it, a stick-on indicator, or a fan of yellow polypropylene yarn tied to the leader with a slip knot.

The rig, then, consists of a nymph that can be weighted or unweighted, enough split shot to get that nymph to the bottom, and a bright strike indicator high enough up the leader to tell you what your nymph is doing down below.

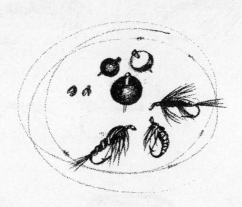

The shot and indicator method works best in water with a fair flow, whether it's a riffle, run, or flat. Fish upstream, or up and across, with short casts: 20′ to 40′. Fish the water you can reach with short casts from one position, then move to a new position, rather than casting long.

Constantly adjust the number of shot and the depth of the indicator, in order to keep the fly on the bottom as you move from one current speed and water depth to another. Your drift should tick bottom on nearly every cast. Start with the indicator about twice the depth of the water up the leader from the fly. In a fast current push it up; in a creeping current move it closer to the fly. The key is constant adjustment as you move to water with different depths and current speeds.

Because trout might be anywhere down there, it's necessary to set up a pattern to cover all of the water. Make your first cast straight upstream, fish it out, then make each subsequent cast a foot farther out. Cover the bottom as if the fly were a paint brush, and your task to lay down stroke after stroke on the bottom, each one directly alongside the one before it.

HOOKING FISH WHILE SHOT AND INDICATOR NYMPHING

There are three parts to successfully setting the hook while nymphing deep: line control, detecting the take, and setting the hook.

Line Control.

Keep the line as straight as you can between the rod tip and the indicator. Hold the rod high to lift line off the water. Flick small mends upstream and down as the line crosses conflicting currents, to keep the line straight. But don't let the line pull on the indicator; it should drift downstream like a dry fly, unrestrained, to give the nymph a natural drift. Strip line in as the indicator approaches your position; feed line out as the indicator passes you and drifts downstream.

Detecting Takes.

Sometimes the indicator dives like a bobber dangled above a worm. More often, the movement is subtle: a slight dip, a 2″ to 3″ dart, or some small hesitation in the indicator's drift, in contradiction to the movement of water surrounding the indicator. Set the hook to any variation in its drift. As you become attuned to this kind of fishing, you'll eventually find yourself successfully setting the hook even though you can't say what prompted you to set it.

Setting the Hook.

Whenever you see any sign of a take, strike instantly. By the time you notice a take up top, it's almost over down below. The trout is about to spit the nymph out. But don't strike so hard that you break off. Instead, use line control to stay in position to merely lift the rod higher and pull the hook home. Lots of times you'll set the hook on bottom bumps. That means you're fishing just right.

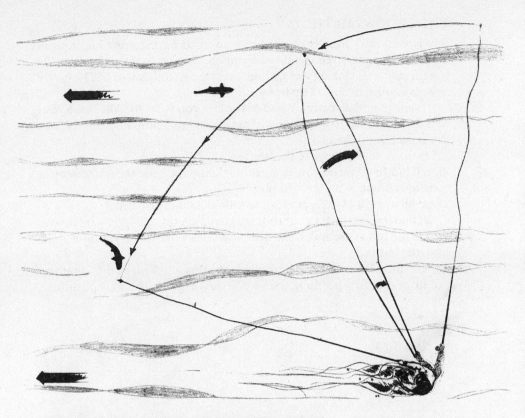

FISHING THE UNENCUMBERED NYMPH

Fishing the split shot and indicator method can be difficult—all those trinkets on the leader tend to tangle. But you can take trout by just tying a weighted nymph to the end of your dry fly leader.

Nymph on the Swing.

In a typical riffle or run, 2′ to 4′ deep, cast 10′ to 15′ upstream from straight across. Let the nymph sink for the first 20′ or so of it's drift, then let the line tighten slightly and begin to lead the nymph downstream and around below you. If it gets going fast, make mends to slow it down.

Upstream Nymph.

Sometimes when trout appear to be taking adult insects off the surface, they're actually feeding on rising nymphs just below it. If you can't fool rising trout with a dry, try fishing an unweighted nymph upstream to the rises, exactly as you would the dry. If your line tip darts, set the hook.

THE BROOKS METHOD

The late Charles Brooks prescribed a method for catching big trout in strong runs, with large weighted nymphs. Use a stout 9' rod, a 7# to 9# weight extra-fast sinking wet-tip line. Keep the leader to 4' or 5'. The heavy nymph should be size #8 up to #4.

Wade in at the upstream end of the run you want to fish. Make your first cast short, 20' to 30', and nearly straight upstream. Fish out the cast in five steps as follows:

1. Let the nymph plunge to the bottom.
2. As it tumbles toward you, draw in slack line and raise the rod to keep in constant contact with the nymph.
3. As the nymph passes you, turn to follow it downstream.
4. Let line out and lower your rod as the nymph tumbles away from you.
5. Stop the rod at the end of the drift and let the line lift the nymph away from the bottom.

Lob the next cast a foot or so outside the first one. Fish all the water you can from your first position, then wade downstream to a new position.

COVERING THE WATER

When nymphing, you're after trout holding down where you can't see them. Boulders, trenches, and other features that form holding lies are not often visible. It's important to cover all of the potential holding water in a disciplined fashion, to give all trout an opportunity to see and whack your nymph as it tumbles past them.

The best way to be sure you cover all of the water is to take up a casting position, then cover what water you can reach from that position with casts that blanket the water, each 1' to 2' from the one before it. Don't move until you've covered all the water you can reach easily from the first position. But don't stretch your casts past about 40'. Beyond that it's difficult to detect takes, and to set the hook. It's best, instead, to wade into a new position that covers new water with shorter casts.

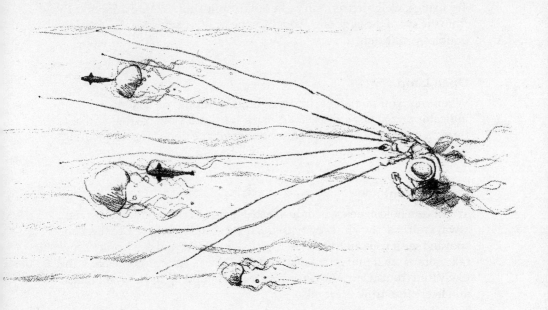

NYMPH TIPS

Try Small Nymphs.

Most folks use size #10 or #12 nymphs. The average size bite a trout eats on the bottom is imitated by a #16. Once you've mastered getting your nymph down on the bottom and drifting freely, the next best thing you can do to improve your nymphing is to use smaller flies.

Two Fly Setups.

Try adding a second nymph to your leader, a different color or size than the first. Tie it to a 10″ to 12″ tippet section, and knot it to the eye of the first fly.

Big Nymph as Weight.

Try using a weighted nymph rather than split shot. Extend a smaller fly from the eye of the large one. It doubles the trout's choices, and sometimes doubles your catch.

Open Loop.

Whenever you're fishing big weighted nymphs, or casting with an indicator and shot on the leader, use a long and slow casting stroke to throw a wide loop. You're not after distance; the open loop keeps things from tangling in the air.

Pods of Trout.

Trout often hold in dense pods in a restricted spot on the bottom. You can't always tell exactly why they're there. If you catch a fish, cast to the same spot and see if you catch another. If you've hit a pod, and catch quite a few, take note of what the water looks like right there. You can come back and likely find trout again. You can go upstream or down, find a similar place, and likely find trout there, also.

Floating Line.

If you can find a way to get your nymph to the bottom while using a floating line, do it. The floater enhances your control over the drift of the nymph. It also serves as an indicator of takes. A sinking line subtracts from control, and reduces the chance that you'll detect a take when you get one.

WET FLY FISHING

Our fishing forefathers fished with nothing but wet flies. The dry fly, and then the advent of nymphs, swept wets aside. Now few folks use them. It's a mistake. Wet flies still resemble a lot of the natural foods that trout eat: drowned mayfly duns, rising caddis pupae, caddis adults swimming down to the bottom to deposit their eggs, even terrestrial insects such as beetles and ants that fall to the water and drown. Wet flies still fool lots of trout that can't be coaxed to other types of flies.

Wet flies should have a place in your fly boxes, and wet fly fishing should play a part in your range of fly fishing skills.

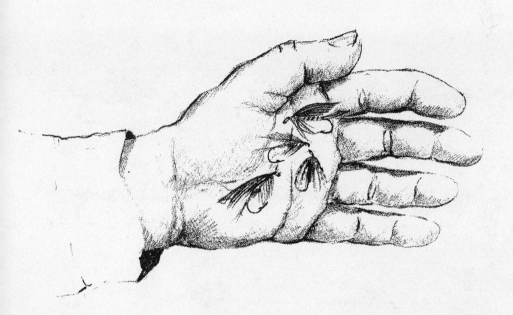

A LIST OF EFFECTIVE WET FLIES

Leadwing Coachman (#10-#14), Light Cahill (#12-#16), McGinty (#10-#12)

Partridge & Yellow (#10-#16), March Brown Spider (#10-#16), Pheasant Tail (#10-#16)

Little Olive Flymph (#14-#18), March Brown Flymph (#12-#16)

Black Wooly Worm (#8-#12), Olive Wooly Worm (#8-#12)

Wet flies come in three different styles: traditional winged wets, wingless wets (sometimes called *flymph,* and soft-hackled wet flies. The following list of effective patterns has samples of each. The following pages show you ways of fishing each kind of fly to take trout.

WET FLY SWING

This ancient method is often denigrated as mere *chuck-and-chance-it*. That's foolish. The reason it worked so well for our fishing forefathers was that it presented wet flies to trout in the same way that nature presents natural insects to them: tossed onto the water and tumbled along by the currents.

The wet fly swing works with any wet fly, but is perhaps best when you're fishing traditional winged wets. Merely cast quartering down and across, and fish the fly around on the swing. The faster the current, the farther downstream you must cast to slow the swing of the fly. The slower the current, the farther upstream you should cast to speed the swing. Try to make the fly swing at about the speed a natural insect might swim. Use line mends to slow it or speed it.

Set up a casting pattern that covers all of the water. Make a cast, fish it out, wade a step, cast again.

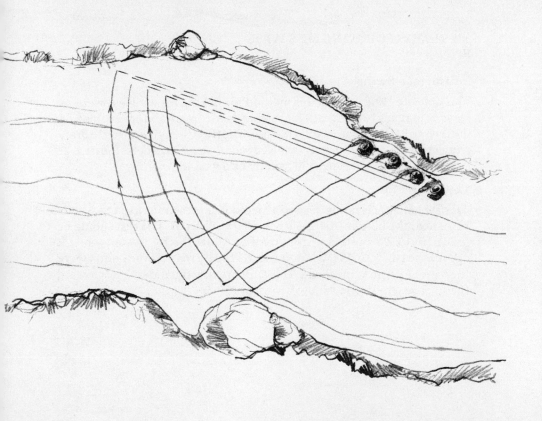

METHODS FOR WINGLESS WETS

Subsurface Swing.

The late Pete Hidy created this method for fishing his wingless wets, or *flymphs,* to rising trout. It calls for casting downstream and across, placing the fly 2' to 3' above and beyond the rise. The fly is then given a tug to draw it under water, after which it is allowed merely to swing across the nose of the feeding trout. The take will usually be a visible swirl.

Leisenring Lift.

The late James Leisenring devised a method for presenting a sparse wet fly on or near the bottom, to the suspected lie of a trout. The cast should be made 10' to 20' upstream from the lie. Allow the fly to sink while it approaches the fish. Just when you think the fly reaches the point where the fish can see it, stop the rod. This animates the fly, and swims it toward the surface. Trout won't allow it to escape.

SOFT-HACKLE SWING

Sylvester Nemes, in his book *The Soft-Hackled Fly*, brought these effective flies back from obscurity. They are easy to tie, and they fool lots of trout because they look like lots of things that trout eat. They're as easy to fish as they are to tie.

Fish soft-hackled wets with the wet fly swing. But cast slightly upstream from your wading position. Let the fly drift idly downstream as long as you can, then use mend after mend to slow the swing of the fly as it comes around below you. As with traditional wets, set up a disciplined rhythm of cast and step, cast and step, to cover all of the water.

Soft-hackled wets fish best in shallow water with a modest to strong current and bottom with boulders. That translates into rocky riffles and runs, studded with stones, and 2' to 4' deep.

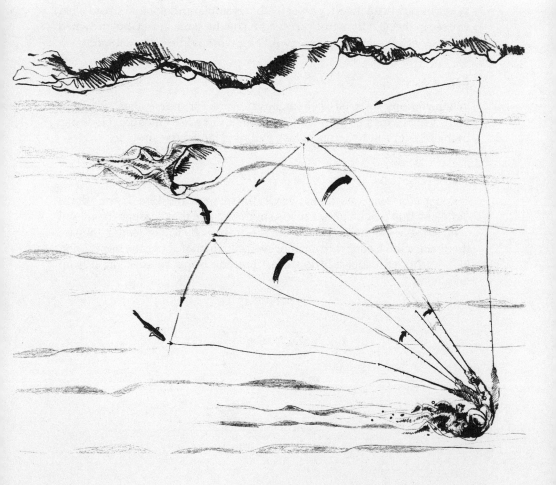

WET FLY TIPS

Setting the Hook.

Trout intercept wets as the flies drift and swing on the current. Sometimes the take is a thud and the trout is hooked for you. Most times, however, the take is a soft tap or tug. Resist the urge to set the hook. You'll just pull it away from the fish. Do nothing; let the fish hook itself.

Simplicity of Wet Fly Gear.

If you're already fishing a dry fly, and want to switch to a wet fly, just nip off the dry and tie on the wet. You're rigged and ready to fish.

Fly Selection.

When insects are active, try a wet fly that is similar in color and size to what you see in the air. Often trout are feeding on the same insect, but drowned and beneath the surface. A wet will then work while a dry will not.

Effective Wets.

When you buy wets, or tie them, always look for sparse ones, with thin bodies, slim wings, and light hackles. Thick, dense wet flies don't look like living insects when they're awash in the water. Sparse ones do.

Two Fly Setups.

It's often advantageous to fish two wet flies at the same time. Try one that's dark, one that's light, or one that's small and one that's larger. Trout will soon tell you which they prefer. Tie the dropper fly to a 6″ leader, then tie this to the main leader with an improved clinch knot above the tippet knot. Use a dropper leader a little stiffer than the tippet to keep them from tangling.

STREAMER FISHING

Streamers are tied to resemble baitfish: minnows and sculpins. They are also great for leeches. All of these food forms offer big bites to trout. It's not difficult to guess the kind of fish you're most likely to catch when you fish streamers: big ones, since they need the largest prey for their daily fuel.

Streamers are traditionally considered best for fishing in spring, when the water is high and cloudy. That is a good time to fish large, heavily weighted flies: size #2 to #6. But for a change in your chances, try this: when the water is low and clear in summer and fall, fish a small unweighted streamer, size #8 to #14. You'll be surprised at the size trout that will chase it, even in thin water.

For the largest streamers, use stout gear: 9' rods that propel 7# to 9# weight lines. Use your heavy. But for smaller streamers, use your normal dry fly gear, even if it's your light. Don't change a thing. That's part of what makes fishing with small streamers so attractive. That and the size fish that you catch.

A LIST OF STREAMERS THAT TAKE TROUT

Black Nose Dace (#2-#8), Mickey Finn (#2-#12)

Little Brook Trout (#4-#8), Spruce (#2-#14)

Muddler (#2-#12), Spuddler (#2-#8)

Matuka (#2-#10), Zonker (#2-#8)

Olive or Black Wooly Bugger (#2-#12), Black or White Marabou Muddler (#2-#10)

THE STREAMER SWING

The basic streamer method is based on the old wet fly swing: *chuck-and-chance-it*. There are real reasons, far removed from chance, that the method works well with streamers. It makes a streamer look like a baitfish swimming madly to escape a trout on its tail.

Make the initial cast across stream, adjusting it slightly up or down depending on the current speed, to get the swing you want. Give the streamer a few feet of drift to sink freely, then draw the line tight and let it lead the fly down and across the current. Because minnows swim faster than insects, you can fish the fly faster than a wet.

As a helpful variation, every other cast or so, set up a rhythmic pulsing of the rod tip. This swims the fly in darts, and might coax trout that refuse the standard swing. Now step and cast, step and cast, covering all the water down a riffle, run, or pool.

FISHING A STREAMER TO BANK WATER

Lots of the largest trout like to stay along undercut banks, where the water is deep and dark and they are sheltered from predators. Sweep a streamer along such a bank, and you're likely to draw them out. The key is to position yourself so that you can cast the fly tight to the bank, and then keep it there as long as possible.

You'll usually find a faster current line between your casting position and the deep bank, so you've got to wade out as near as you can to this faster water. Cast over it, then hold as much line up out of it as you can, to keep it from putting a belly in the line.

Make your cast slightly upstream from straight across. Let the fly swim unhindered down along the bank. Toss upstream mends often to keep the current from drawing the streamer away from the bank. Once the fly does draw out, then fish it across the entire current on a normal streamer swing.

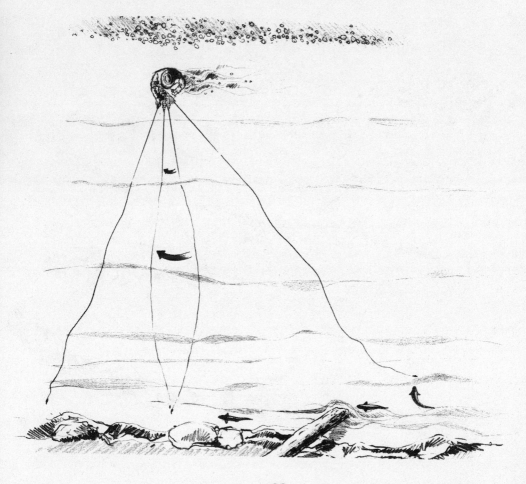

THE BOTTOM BOUNCE

Big trout often hold along the bottom in pools and deep runs. If you can get a streamer down to them and thud it along the bottom, they'll usually take it with a thump.

The secret is to use an extra-fast sinking wet-tip or wet-belly line, with a 4′ to 5′ leader and heavily weighted streamer. Make your casts upstream at an angle across the current. Give the fly lots of time to get down to the bottom. Then mend line, and even feed line into the drift of the fly, doing all you can to keep it there, bouncing along.

THE TACTIC OF CHANGE

People new to trout fishing make a common mistake: they get rooted to one spot, doing one thing, and fail to change even when they fail to catch trout. Here's a logical sequence of change to bump yourself into whenever the fishing gets poor.

Fly Pattern.

Change to a fly in the same style you're already using—dry, wet, streamer, or nymph—but a smaller one, larger one, darker one, or lighter one.

Presentation.

Try changing the direction from which you approach a lie and cast to it. Read the water carefully for conflicting currents. Then take the best position to present the type fly you're fishing.

Type of Fly.

If you're not catching fish on dries, switch to wets or nymphs. Often when they appear to be feeding on the surface, trout are actually taking something just beneath it.

Depth.

Try changing the depth at which you fish your fly. If it's a wet or streamer, switch to a wet-tip or wet-belly line. If it's a nymph—this is most important with nymphs—add a split shot or two on the leader, or slip the strike indicator up a foot or two. Often such a slight change will suddenly fill the water with fish.

Water Fished.

If you've fished awhile in one spot and haven't hooked anything lately, no matter what else you change, then move on. You've probably worn the place out, put the fish off their feed.

Water Type.

Try a different water type: switch from riffles to pools, or from runs to bank water. Find the water type where the trout are holding, then concentrate on it.

Stream Fished.

If the stream you're on is not producing, hasn't for a long time, and doesn't promise to soon, then try going somewhere else. Fishing might be hot in the next watershed over.

READING TROUT WATER

It has often been said that 10 percent of the fishermen catch 90 percent of the fish. That is extreme, but some fly fishermen take lots more trout than others. The critical skill that elevates them is not the fancy rods that they fish, nor their casting ability. It is simply their ability to read water and find fish. They fish water that contains trout. They spend little time fishing water that doesn't.

Reading water is merely a matter of noticing where a stream meets the basic needs of trout: protection from predators, shelter from strong currents, and food. Locate places where these three things are available, and you've likely found trout. In the following pages we'll look at stream structure, the different kinds of trout lies, and then the various water types—riffles, runs, pools, flats—that hold fish, and where you're most likely to find them.

Recall, as you read on, that the essential way to learn to read water is to catch fish, and then to remember what the water looked like where you caught them.

STRUCTURE OF A STREAM

A typical trout stream slowly erodes its course into a series of bends. Sometimes these bends form in soft curves, other times they're sharp turns, but often they're gentle meanders. As it forms its wandering course, a stream repeats certain kinds of structures. These are *riffles, runs, rapids, pools, flats,* and *bank water.*

If you learn where the trout hold in each of these water types, and learn the best ways to approach those trout, then you'll begin catching lots more of them.

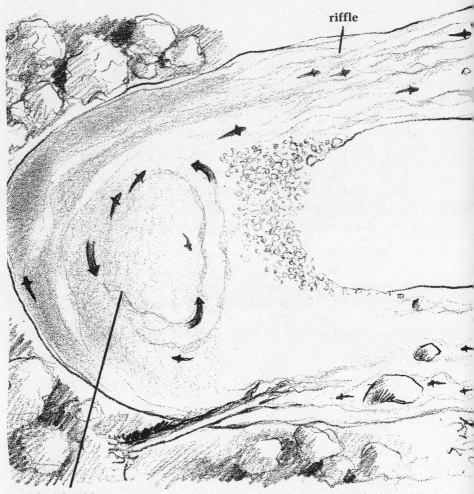

riffle

pool with eddy

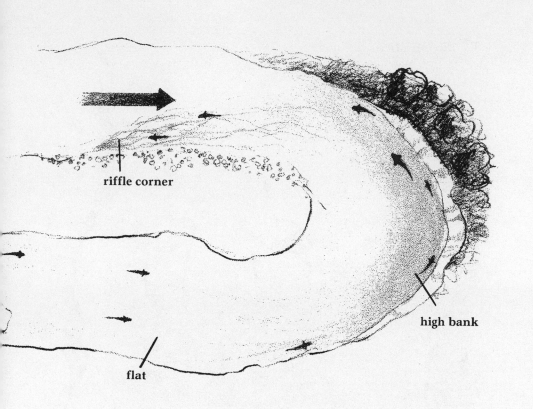

riffle corner

high bank

flat

brushy bank

pocket water

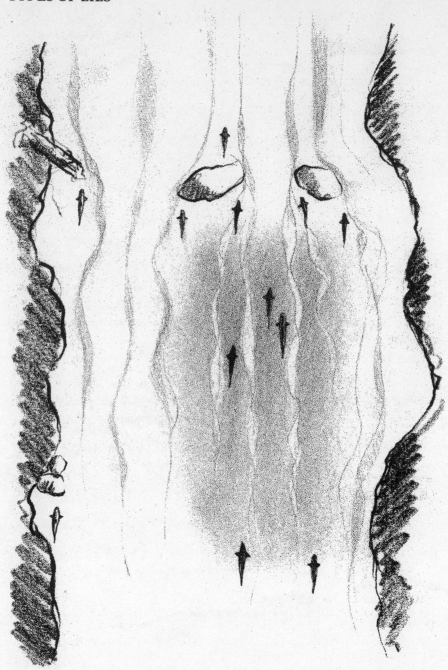

Holding Lie.

This kind of lie offers protection from predators and shelter from currents, usually in the form of depth, or a boulder, log, ledge, or trench. Some food gets delivered on the current. Trout spend most of their time on holding lies, moving out to feeding lies whenever more food is available there.

Feeding Lie.

Trout move to feeding lies, usually on a flat or in a riffle, whenever insects or some other food form becomes active and available. Trout are often vulnerable to predation on feeding lies, and ignore the danger in their greed to feed, but head back to their holding lies as soon as the food disappears.

Prime Lie.

This is the kind of lie where everything comes together in one place: protection from predators, shelter from strong currents, and lots of food. Usually such a lie forms above or below a boulder in a run or flat, or in a pool where an incoming current delivers food into the protective depths down below. Converging current seams, where food gets gathered, often form prime lies. Wherever you find a prime lie, you're likely to find a prime trout, the hefty kind you'd most like to catch.

Sheltering Lies.

These have been referred to as *bomb shelters.* They are places where the trout go when they've been frightened out of other lies. A sheltering lie is usually deep, dark, and absolutely protected from everything. It might be down in the depths of a pool, or far back beneath a log jam. Such lies are rarely rich in food, so sheltering lies are not always occupied unless the trout are in retreat . . .except for an occasional old predaceous lunker that makes its living by intercepting smaller fish busy diving into hiding.

THE FOUR DEPTHS AT WHICH TROUT FEED

No matter what kind of water you fish, trout can be found feeding at one of four levels in the water, depending on where they find most of their food at the moment. You'll want to develop an awareness of the level at which trout feed. It's too easy to fish on top with dries when trout are working the bottom for nymphs, or to fish nymphs when trout have their attention riveted up top. If you present your fly at the level where trout are concentrated, you're bound to catch more of them.

Bottom.

Aquatic insects and most other trout food forms spend much of their lives on the bottom. They are available higher in the water column only when they make their dash to the top for emergence. As a consequence, trout spend most of their time on or near the bottom, where bits of food are constantly delivered to them. If you see no signs that trout are elsewhere, assume they're feeding at the bottom. Fish for them there.

Mid-Depths.

Mayfly nymphs and caddis pupae must get from the bottom to the top before the adult can emerge and fly away. To get to the top, these insects must pass through the mid-depths. Trout sometimes suspend between the bottom and the top to feed there. If you find yourself in a hatch of caddis or mayflies, you've tried dries and you've tried nymphs, often a switch to a wet fly fished a foot or two deep will be well rewarded.

Subsurface.

Many aquatic insect forms rise to the top, then get pinned under the surface film, where their numbers become concentrated. Trout take them within inches of the top. The take sends a swirl to the surface, and it's easy to mistake subsurface feeding for trout taking on top. Watch to see if any naturals disappear in the swirls; look for a bubble of air left in the rise-ring. If you don't see either, assume subsurface feeding and try a suspended nymph or a wet fly on a slow swing.

Surface.

Of course trout often feed right on top, with visible takes. When they're doing this, it's dry fly time, probably everybody's favorite moment. But don't overlook the top even when trout are on the bottom. If the water is shallow enough, say 2' to 4' deep, trout can still be coaxed to the top when you don't see any sign that they're feeding there.

READING AND FISHING RIFFLES

Riffles are shallow, generally 1′ to 4′ deep. Their rough surfaces reflect cobble and stones on the bottom below. The current is usually brisk. Trout are found in such fast water only where they find some obstruction to the current, or when so many insects hatch that it's worthwhile to leave a holding lie and fight the current.

Very fast and shallow riffles that lack any sheltering obstructions rarely hold trout. These types of riffles are *empty water*. Your take of trout will increase instantly if you learn to read empty water, and avoid wasting time in it.

Trout nearly always hold on the bottom in riffles. But the water is shallow, so they are able to see any type of fly that passes near them: a nymph on the bottom, a wet fly at mid-depths, or a dry floating on the nearby surface. They would not be in the riffle if they were not feeding; they will usually be willing to dash after any type of fly you present to them.

Methods that are most effective in riffles include the searching dry fly fished with upstream casts, the wet fly or soft-hackle fished on the swing, or the nymph fished deep with split shot and strike indicator.

PATTERNING A RIFFLE

Riffles have many promising holding lies that are visible: boulders, ledges, and trenches. But they also have many more that are not visible. You cannot see every feature on the bottom that breaks the current and provides a possible lie for a trout.

Keep this fact in mind when you fish a riffle with any method. Be sure to cover all of the water with your casts. Of course you want to concentrate your effort where you see an obvious prime lie. But don't neglect the rest of the water, because trout tend to be sprinkled throughout riffles. Set up a disciplined casting pattern, and cover all of the water.

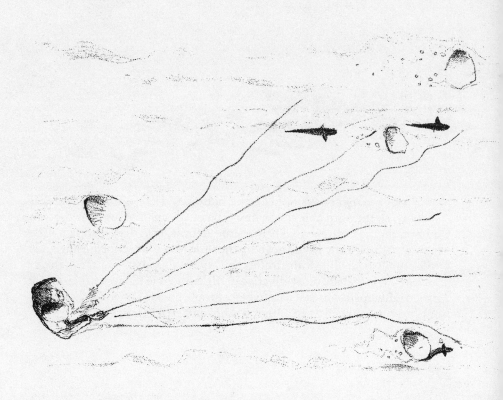

RIFFLE CORNERS

Wherever a fast and chatty riffle breaks over a gravel shelf into slightly deeper water downstream, it forms one of a stream's prime lies: a riffle corner. The shallow water above is usually too brisk to hold fish. The forceful water outside the shelf usually has too few current obstructions to allow trout to hold in it. But the water right at the edge, along the current seam between fast water and slow, is almost always deep enough to protect fish from overhead predation, and slow enough to shelter them from the current. All of the food washed down from the productive riffle above makes it a prime lie.

Fish these corners by dancing a dry fly down the current seam. Or use the split shot and indicator technique to dangle a nymph or two down the line between fast water and slow. Fish both of these methods from downstream, wading and working up into the very corner itself.

It's also effective to wade in above the corner, then cast a wet fly, or better a brace of them, onto the fast water outside the corner. Let this team swing around into the slower water, where trout wait to intercept insects in distress.

READING AND FISHING RUNS

Runs tend to be deeper than riffles, and their bottoms are less cobbled, so their tops are less rough. The gradient in a run is not as steep, so the current is generally less brisk, though still strong. In small creeks, runs vary from 1½' to 4' deep. In typical trout streams they are 3' to 6' deep. In the largest rivers, a run might be from 3' to 10' deep.

Most runs have a riffle at the head, then gradually slow and deepen downstream. Many of them lift up at the lower end to drop off into the next riffle; others pause and deepen to become pools. More boulders lodge in runs than in riffles; these break the current, and provide plenty of holding lies for trout. Unlike riffles, trout hold in runs even when no food form is active. Like riffles, trout tend to remain on the bottom in runs unless a hatch draws them upward

Methods that work best in runs are usually those that get the fly right to the bottom, except at times when trout are actively feeding up near the top. In shallow runs, say less than 4' deep, trout will sometimes hold on the bottom but move to the top for a dry fly. But in deeper water, trout will not normally rise to take a dry unless they're already holding high in the water column. A wet fly or streamer that gets down a foot or two will often coax them up. But the most effective method is the split shot and indicator technique for fishing nymphs.

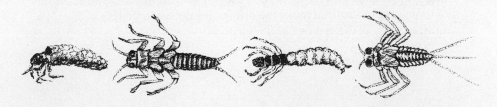

FISHING LIKELY LIES IN RUNS

Trout in runs hold most often around obstructions: above and below boulders, in the shelter of logs breaking the current, or in trenches where the bottom is deeper and slower than the water around it. Not all of these lies are always easy to see, and it often pays to fish a run the same way you do a riffle: by patterning the water to cover all of the bottom. But reading water and finding potential lies can eliminate a lot of unproductive water in runs, and save you lots of fishing time.

Look for boils on the surface that reflect boulders down below. Look for dark slicks on an otherwise bumpy surface, reflecting a place where the bottom falls away into a trench, a prime lie for lots of trout. Fish these places carefully with nymphs, and be sure to adjust your weight and indicator so the nymphs get right to the bottom. Sometimes the addition of a single split shot can make the difference between no fish at all and a sudden spate of them when you hit a pod.

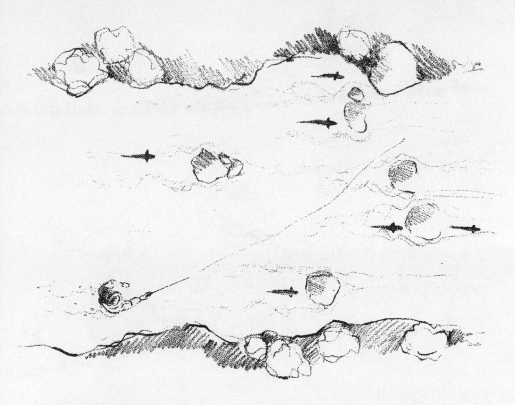

POCKET WATER

Some runs border on being rapids, and in most places have currents too fast to allow trout to rest and feed. But inside this tumbling water, you can usually find a few places where the current is broken, and water builds up in front of a boulder or eddies behind it. Trout find holding lies in these pockets. They hover along the bottom and dash out to intercept whatever the current rushes past.

You can fish pocket water by dropping a large dry fly onto the top of it. Let it dance until it coaxes something up. Or wade upstream from the pocket, and swing a streamer or brace of wet flies in front of the obstruction and behind it. The best way to entice trout out of a pocket might be with a large weighted nymph, fished on an 8' to 10' leader and a floating line. Just pop the nymph into the pocket and allow it to sink.

No matter what method you choose to probe pockets, be sure to fish with the shortest line possible. Because the water is so broken, you can get right up onto the fish without frightening them. Make your casts 15' to 25', hold your rod high to lift the line off the water, and you'll have maximum control over your presentation.

READING AND FISHING POOLS

Pools are places where a creek, stream, or river slows and deepens. They are obvious sheltering lies; trout flee into these *bomb shelters* when they've been frightened off their normal lies. There they find the protection of depth and darkness.

But not all trout found in pools are there because they've been scared away from someplace else. The ecology of a pool attracts larger life forms—crayfish and baitfish—and therefore becomes the one best spot for the largest trout in any stream to find the larger bites that it needs to sustain itself. Pools are the obvious prime lies for the biggest trout you're likely to find along the course of any trout stream.

The size of a pool is relative to the size of the stream. In a tiny creek, a plunge pool might be 3' deep, 5' wide, 10' long. In a typical trout stream, a pool will more likely be 6' to 10' deep, 20' to 30' wide, up to 100' long. In the largest trout rivers, pools might be 15' to 20' deep, too wide to cast across, long enough that you need a boat to ply their lengths.

The best methods for pools are obviously those that get your flies down into that depth and darkness. Use streamers and weighted nymphs. If the stream, and therefore the pool, is of any size, use fast-sinking or extra-fast sinking wet-tip and wet-head lines to get the flies down.

THE BEND POOL

The typical trout stream works its course into a series of curves, so the bend pool becomes one of the most common types. The force of the current is directed toward the outside edge of a bend pool, so the water tends to be deepest there, shallowest on the inside. Trout generally lie in the deepest part of any stretch of stream. You usually want to fish the deep outer edge of a bend pool.

If the bend pool is narrow enough to cast across and shallow enough that trout will rise to its surface, you can fish upstream with dries. If the pool requires a long cast to cross, and the water is deeper than about 4', it's best to fish bend pools downstream with wet flies, streamers, or weighted nymphs.

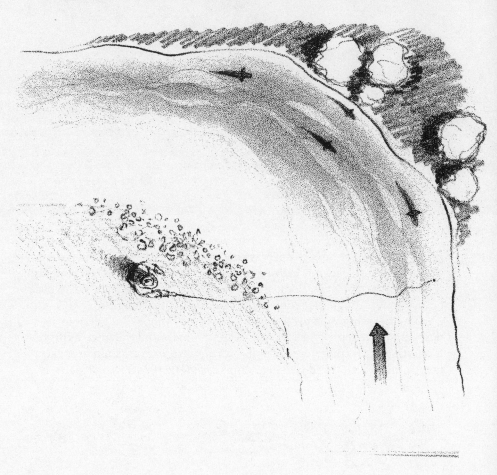

PLUNGE POOLS

Plunge pools form wherever the water tumbles over an obstruction, eroding a hole into the bottom below. The obstruction might be a waterfall, resulting in a deep and spreading fan pool. Or it might be a smaller drop, resulting in a pool of more normal proportions for the size of the stream it's in. All of these plunge pools hold trout because they offer shelter from the current and protection from predators.

In tiny streams, it's best to fish plunge pools with dry flies danced on top. Cast them right to the edges of the froth and foam. Let them float as long as they will. In larger pools, with water more than 4' to 6' deep, it might take awhile for trout to get coaxed into the rush to the top.

In big and deep plunge pools, try weighted nymphs tossed right into the drop. The downrushing water will carry the fly down with it, then deliver it into the current surging along the bottom. That is where trout wait for their food to be delivered in plunge pools.

FISHING EDDY POOLS

Eddies form wherever the current, rushing or idling down a river or stream, glances off a point of land and turns a circle behind the point. These eddies make natural gathering points for all the little lives that find themselves awash on the current.

   If trout are feeding on those lives at or near the surface of an eddy, try taking them with small nymphs or soft-hackled wet flies fished just under the surface film. Because of conflicting currents, it's difficult to get a good presentation with a dry fly. But a fly fished inches deep will look like something alive, trying to swim to the surface.

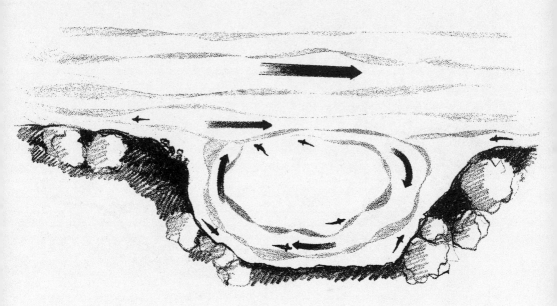

POOL CORNERS

Many pools have prime lies where a riffle rushes in, then slows down and deepens. Because the riffle delivers food, trout crowd right at the corners, where they can hold easily and dash out to intercept what the current offers.

If the corner is shallow you can fish it with dry flies. It also works well to cast a wet fly, or a pair of them, into the fast current outside the corner, then swim it into the slow water at the corner. If the water is 4' or deeper, it's usually best to fish a nymph upstream along the current seam between fast water and slow. Use split shot to get to the bottom and an indicator to tell you about takes.

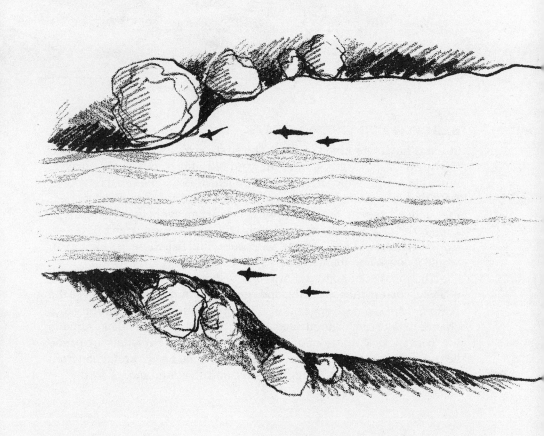

READING AND FISHING FLATS

Streams have two kinds of flats. The first is shallow and rather swift, flowing over a rocky bottom. This kind of flat is rough on the surface, much like a riffle, which it resembles in all but the steepness of its gradient. A flat of this type can be surprisingly barren of trout, especially if it is less than 2' deep and has few places where trout can avoid the brisk current and overhead predation. If you find obstructions to the current, however, trout will find holding lies there, and you should fish these lies just as you would if you found them in a riffle.

The most common kind of flat is deeper, 3' to 5', and has a more peaceful current than the riffles and runs above and below it. Because the bottom is not scoured, deposits of silt form, and aquatic vegetation gets a chance to take root. The surface, reflecting the bottom, is slick. Aquatic life, because of the vegetation, is abundant. These gentle flats are prime lies for trout because they provide their three main needs: protection from predators, shelter from strong currents, and an abundance of food.

The vegetation on these gentle flats provides millions of miniature niches for aquatic insects and crustaceans. Most of the insects tend toward the smallest sizes: size #16 to #20 mayflies, #14 to #18 caddis, and #18 to #24 midges. The best fishing on flats is usually done with small flies fished at two levels, the bottom and the top, with one of two methods: the imitative dry fly, or the nymph fished with split shot and strike indicator.

READING AND FISHING BANK WATER

About 75 percent of bank water is empty water. Fish it all and you're wasting most of your time. Instead, look for three things: current, depth, and an obstruction, and fish only where you find all three together.

Current.

Good bank water has a current sufficient to deliver food. Remember this: no current, no food, no trout.

Depth.

Bank water that holds trout drops off fast enough to give protection from overhead predation. If the water at the edge slopes abruptly to 2' to 4' deep, it will hold trout.

Obstructions.

A current is required to deliver food, but trout can't hold against it for long. So they need undercuts, indentations, or boulders to break the current. Find these obstructions, and you've found the trout.

The upstream dry fly is excellent along banks. Rock hop along the same bank you fish. Use an attractor pattern, such as an Elk Hair Caddis or Royal Wulff. Place it within a foot of the bank; fishing 5' out is an excellent way to get some exercise.

FLY FISHING SMALL CREEKS

The higher up its watershed you go, the more boisterous a stream gets. Some small creeks meander through flatlands, but most are found in foothills and mountains. They plunge and bound from pool to pool, with few of the longer riffles and runs of more mature streams.

Brush hanging overhead often chokes a creek and restricts the cast. Small creeks call for short rods: 7' to 8' long. Most aquatic and terrestrial insects found in and along small waters are fairly large, so the flies you'll cast will be searching dries and nymphs in sizes #10 to #16. These call for 4- and 5-weight lines, nothing lighter.

Tactics on tiny waters call for hiking and fishing upstream, whether you're fishing the surface or the bottom. The creeks are too narrow to cast across, and it's difficult to present the fly adrift and drag-free when moving downstream. Constant upstream movement is the key. Once you've taken a few casts over a pool, and shown the fly to all the trout there, move on. The biggest mistake you can make on a tiny stream is to get rooted in one spot.

FISHING AVERAGE TROUT STREAMS

Most average-sized trout streams have riffles, runs, and pools repeated along their length. Streams erode their courses in a series of curves, so the pools often form at a bend, with deep undercut banks along the outside.

Tackle for medium-sized streams naturally falls in the center of the selection; if you've chosen a 3-rod battery your medium will be perfect. If you choose to buy just one rod, it should suit this kind of fishing, because it is the kind that most of us do most of the time. An 8½' to 9' rod balanced to a 5- or 6-weight line would be perfect.

As you move upstream or down, fishing a medium-sized trout stream, you'll encounter all kinds of water, and will want to be prepared to fish them all. This is where becoming skilled in reading water, and then knowing how to best approach and fish potential lies, pay the highest premiums.

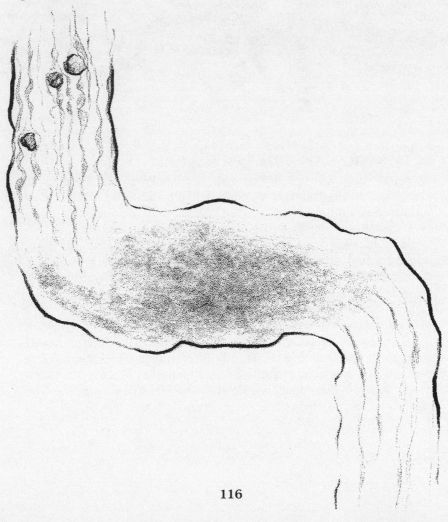

FISHING LARGE RIVERS

A large river can seem formidable at first. It looks so big that it seems you could never figure out where to fish it. But all you've got to do is break it down into its parts, and it becomes quite simple. Just look for riffles, runs, pools, and flats with the features that meet the needs of trout.

At first glance your heaviest gear seems right for fishing the largest of streams. This is true if you are drifting in a boat, pounding the banks with weighted nymphs and streamers. But it's not true if you're wading the water and fishing riffles and flats, which is most likely. You fish them exactly as you would on smaller water, and with the same gear. Your light outfit, an 8' to 9' rod for a 4- to 5-weight line, is perfect unless the wind is blowing, in which case you might want your medium.

A drift boat or raft gives you an advantage on large rivers. You can fish the banks as you drift along. But more important, it delivers you from riffle to distant riffle, or flat to flat, making it easy to find the fish.

MEADOW STREAMS AND SPRING CREEKS

Meadow streams and spring creeks tend to have gentle gradients and meandering courses. They nose from bend to bend, nudge at lots of undercut banks. They have few riffles and runs. Because the current is slow, and not subject to spring scour, their bottoms often become layered with soil, where vegetation takes root and trails up toward a smooth surface.

The combination of smooth currents and lots of vegetation places a premium on matching hatches. Such streams have heavy populations of aquatic insects; such smooth currents cause trout to feed on them selectively. Because the trout are exposed to overhead predation when they come up to feed, they are wary.

Spring creeks and meadow streams are best fished with light gear and delicate presentations with small dry flies and tiny nymphs. Long leaders, 10' to 14', are the rule; fine tippets in the 5X and 6X class are necessary.

Hone your stalking skills for this kind of fishing. Keep that 10-degree line of sight of the trout constantly on your mind. Be patient, move less than you would on other streams, and spend more time watching for working trout. Once you've found them, concentrate on fooling them.

FISHING TAILWATERS

A dam, in certain circumstances, can turn a dirty warmwater river into a cold and clear trout stream. The reservoir behind a dam serves as a giant cooling and settling basin: water chills in the depths, and silt drops to the bottom. The stream below the dam becomes perfect for aquatic insects, and for trout.

Because tailwater flows are tamed, they tend to have smooth currents, rooted vegetation, and heavy hatches of insects. Trout feed selectively, and it's often helpful to match a hatch. Most of the currents are smooth, so trout are wary. Tailwater conditions are usually very similar to spring creeks and meadow streams. You've got to fish them with a similar degree of caution, and with the same delicate gear.

When trout are not up and actively feeding in a tailwater, then try fishing a nymph along the bottom, using the split shot and indicator technique. Be sure to try small flies, size #16 and even #18, because that's the average size of the natural nymphs and larvae that trout see on the bottom of a tailwater.

MATCHING HATCHES

Matching hatches sounds frightening at first. You've got to study Latin, pour over all those textbooks, identify insects to family, genus, and species. It might take a lifetime. But think about this: trout don't speak Latin, they don't read textbooks, and they can't even identify themselves to species. But they make a fine living eating insects.

You can find out everything you need to know about an insect merely by collecting it and observing it. You don't need to identify it. Just take careful note of three things: its size, form, and color. Then select the nearest fly pattern you've got to match it. A small aquarium net, a jar lid with a white interior, a magnifying glass, and a few vials filled with alcohol will aid your collecting and observing. But even they are not necessary.

MATCHING MAYFLIES

Mayflies have three life stages. The first stage, the nymph, lives on bottom stones, or swims and crawls about in vegetation. At rare times trout might take them selectively down there; most of the time they feed on them at random, along with lots of other things. A generic nymph, a small Hare's Ear, Pheasant Tail, or Fox Squirrel, imitates the real thing closely enough.

The second stage, the dun, emerges at the surface. It is the most important stage of the mayfly. Duns resemble little sailboats, and come off in fleets, so trout key on them, and often refuse anything else. Because mayfly duns hatch out in open water, they are very vulnerable to trout. Match them with Compara-duns, traditional Catskill dressings, or Hairwing Duns in the appropriate size and color.

The last stage, the spinner, lays its eggs and falls spent to the water, usually at evening. When clouds of spinners descend, trout key on them, and you've got to match them. You can do it with simple dries that have hackle splayed out to both sides. Most often, however, it's best to fish a sparse wet fly just under the surface.

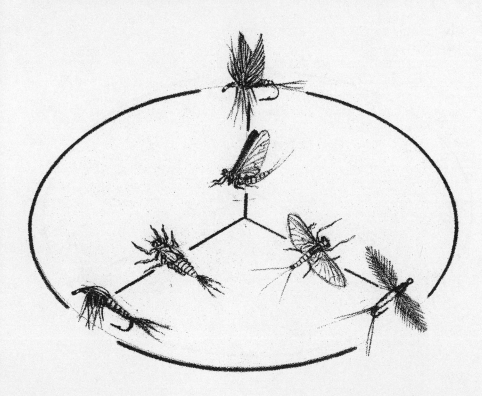

MATCHING CADDIS

Caddisflies also have three important stages. The larval stage lives on bottom stones, or crawls about in rooted vegetation. Most build cases, and are relatively safe from trout. But many stream types—the Green Rock Worms—build no case. These live in riffles, and trout often feed on them. Bright flies such as the Green Caddis Larva should be tumbled right on the bottom in fast water.

Caddis pupae tweezer out of the larval case and dash to the top for emergence. This brief transitional stage is very difficult to observe. When you see caddis dancing in the air over a stream, but cannot catch trout on dry flies, suspect pupae, and fish soft-hackled wets on the swing.

Adult caddis are erratic fliers, difficult for trout to capture. So they often hit them with quick, splashy rises. Try the Elk Hair Caddis or Deer Hair Caddis. Many adult caddis deposit their eggs by swimming under the water. If you see lots of caddis dancing in the air at evening, but again cannot take trout with dries, try a winged wet the same size and color as the adults in the air.

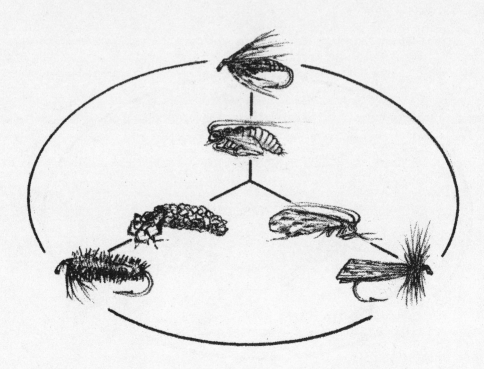

MATCHING STONEFLIES

Stoneflies have only two important stages. The nymphs live on the bottom, usually in water that is charged with lots of oxygen: rapids, riffles, and fast runs. They vary in size from tiny #16 up to giant #4. The most important are the largest. Imitate them with weighted nymphs such as the Kaufmann's Black Stone and Kaufmann's Golden Stone in sizes # 4 to #8. Tumble these right on the bottom.

Adult stoneflies scramble about in streamside vegetation, and make short awkward flights out over the water. They often fall in, and often get taken by trout. Dry flies such as the Sofa Pillow and Stimulator work well in sizes #4 through #10. Fish them dead drift, usually as near to the banks as you can get them.

MATCHING MIDGES

Midges are generally tiny, sizes #16 through #22. Some species in the northern range of trout habitat are as large as size #10. But most are small, and are attractive to trout only when they emerge in great numbers, which they do often. Midges are especially important in spring, fall, and even winter when other insect hatches do not occur.

Midges have two important life stages. The first is the pupa, which ascends slowly to the surface, then hesitates at the surface film before breaking through for emergence into the adult stage. Imitate the pupae with size #14 to #22 TDC nymphs in standard black, or in olive and red color variations. Fish these on a long, fine leader and floating line, up near the surface in smooth water.

The second stage, the adult, is best imitated with patterns such as the Adams or Adams Parachute in the very smallest sizes. A Griffith's Gnat, which is no more than a peacock herl body with grizzly hackle wound over it the length of the hook shank, floats flush in the surface film and represents the adult trying to escape the pupal shuck. Such simple dressings often work alarmingly well during midge hatches.

MATCHING TERRESTRIALS

Trout don't pass up any insects that fall to the water from grass, brush, or trees alongside the stream. Such luckless creatures make up a large part of the trout diet at certain times of the year.

Hoppers.

Grasshoppers get blown into the water on hot and windy summer afternoons. They are important on streams that meander through fields and meadows. Imitate them with patterns such as Joe's Hopper and the Letort Hopper in #8 to #12.

Ants.

Tiny ants get into lots of trouble on trout streams. They're difficult to observe on the water without the aid of an aquarium net. Most pattern books will list dressings for #18 to #22 Black Ants and Cinnamon Ants.

Beetles.

These fall to the stream in a variety of sizes. Those that you want to match will normally be small. Use the Crowe Beetle and Deerhair Beetle in #16 to #20.

Inchworms.

These bright green insects rappel down to streams on their fine silk threads each autumn. Imitate them with bright chenille wound on a size #10 to #14 hook, and fish them wet beneath overhanging branches.

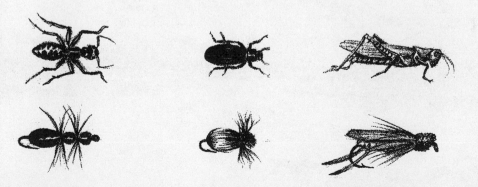

Chapter 6

Fly Fishing for Trout in Lakes

Many folks think lakes are mysteries. They wonder: Where do I find trout in all that vast expanse? A lake looks like a blank slate to them; nothing on its surface seems to speak about anything on its bottom.

In truth, lakes are rather simple. They're not nearly as mysterious nor as difficult to fish as they're made out to be.

Trout in lakes and ponds have almost exactly the same needs that they do in streams. You find them in accordance with the way a stillwater meets those needs. They don't have to fight a current. But they do need protection from predators, so you don't find them up on the surface, where they're exposed to osprey and eagle, except when easy meals attract them there. And they need comfortable temperature and oxygen regimes, so you find them down in the depths, near the cool thermocline, only when the highest heat of summer drives them to it.

Finally, trout need food. Aquatic insects thrive in vegetation. Plants grow only where light strikes. So trout find their food, and you find the trout, in shallows 3' to 10' deep throughout most of the long fishing season.

THE EDGES OF LAKES

Most folks, when fishing lakes, motor or paddle furiously right out toward the middle, where they think the big ones are. Don't make the same mistake. Most of the time, most of the fish are in shallow water, near the edges of the lake.

Photosynthetic growth occurs only in sunlight. Usually it takes the form of weedbeds in the shallows, but it can also often be a thin layer of algae and diatoms down on the bottom. In most trout lakes, sunlight strikes bottom at 10' to 15'. Light penetrates through very clear water to a depth of 25' to 30'. In murky water it might not penetrate more than 5'. Aquatic insects and crustaceans browse along the bottom, or crawl and flit among the leaves of weeds, wherever light strikes. Since trout eat insects and crustaceans, they can nearly always be found at depths where light spurs weed growth.

This tells you where to start fishing in lakes and ponds. Light always reaches the bottom around the edges. So it's no surprise that you'll nearly always do well by fishing the shorelines. If the bottom slopes gently away from shore, you'll find weedbeds, and therefore trout, extending 50' to 100' feet from the edge. If the lake drops off abruptly into deep water, however, you won't often find fish more than 10' to 20' out.

INLETS AND OUTLETS

Trout gather around inlet and outlet streams for a variety of reasons, so these are consistently good places to look for fish. Always approach inlets and outlets quietly and cautiously, and explore them carefully with your flies.

Spawning.

All trout species, with the exception of brookies, need running water in which to spawn. So look for cutthroat and rainbow trout to gather at inlets in spring. Brown trout move to the same places in fall.

Cool Flows.

Shaded streams remain cool in summer, while lake shallows get warm. So trout nose toward creek mouths whenever the water begins to be uncomfortable in late June and July. Later, they move out and down toward the thermocline.

Food.

Whenever a hatch of insects occurs in a stream coming into a lake, trout will edge into the current and feed there. Outlets serve as funnels, concentrating food and coaxing trout.

TROUT MOVEMENT

The movement of trout in lakes takes two primary forms. In *major movements,* they migrate to the edges and shallows in spring, just after ice out, and stay there through early summer. Then they drop out and down into the cool depths in mid-summer, when the water gets hot. They return to the shallows with the first cool days of fall. Finally, when winter chill sets in, trout drop into the depths again and remain there.

Minor movements are the restless wanderings of trout within the area of the major movement. A pod of trout, or even an individual, cruises restlessly along the shoreline, or scours a weedbed, or roams around the delta where a stream enters. Find where the trout prefer to be in a major movement, then intercept them cruising in a minor movement within that area, and you're going to catch one or two each time they pass by.

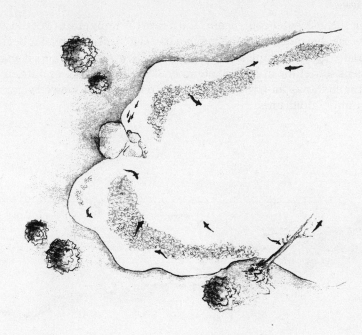

STRATIFICATION AND TURNOVER

Stratification.

Colder water is denser, and therefore sinks to the bottom of the lake. Warmer water is lighter and stays toward the top. In summer the border between warmer water and colder water sometimes becomes abrupt, and is called the *thermocline*. When a distinct thermocline forms, with warm water above and cold water below, the lake is said to be *stratified*. In most trout lakes, the thermocline forms at about 15' to 20' deep. Water above the thermocline circulates with the action of wind and waves, and stays charged with oxygen. Water beneath it becomes stagnant. Trout need oxygen; when a lake is stratified, you'll find them only above the thermocline. If water near the surface gets warm, say a few degrees above 70, then trout drop down toward the cooler thermocline, but do not go below it. So in hot weather, you usually find trout around 15' to 20' deep.

Turnover.

When surface water cools again, and nears the temperature of the water below the thermocline, there comes a day when all of the water begins to circulate, and it tumbles over. This is called *turnover,* and it usually happens sometime in early September. This lifts a surge of nutrients up into the shallows, and trout return there to feed with renewed vigor after the summer doldrums.

SEASONS OF A LAKE

Spring.

The shallows warm first with the new sun, and aquatic life gets active as soon as the ice goes out, or the water begins to warm. Hatches of mayflies, caddisflies, and midges all entice trout out of their winter depths in April, May, and June. Spring is the most exciting time of year to be on lakes. Trout are in water 2' to 10' deep, where it's easy to get at them with fly fishing gear. And they're hungry, eager to whack your flies.

Summer.

Insect hatches continue in early summer: more mayflies and caddis come off, plus damselflies and dragonflies. Trout remain in water less than 10' to 12' deep until warmer water temperatures of mid-simmer cause them to move toward the thermocline to keep cool. Usually this happens in late June in lowland lakes, in July or early August in lakes at higher elevations.

Fall.

Trout remain deep until fall turnover mixes the water, delivering cool water and lots of nutrients back up to the top. Then they move back into shallower water and feed actively. Because insect hatches are less common in September and October, hungry trout are more likely to take larger wet flies and streamers.

Winter.

Few insects are active in winter, and the water is cold. Trout tend to idle their engines, moving little and feeding only occasionally, in November through March. But if the water remains free of ice, and a hatch of winter midges occurs, trout will come right to the top to feed on them. That's the way trout are: whenever food is available, they'll stir themselves and feed on it, no matter the time of year.

EQUIPMENT FOR LAKES

The *medium* outfit described in Chapter 2 is perfect for trout fishing in lakes. An 8½' to 9' rod that carries a 6- or 7-weight line will work for almost all stillwater situations.

Rods.

The need for distance arises often on lakes, and you'll rarely have brush overhead. A long rod is better than a short one. 8½' to 9' rods that are best for streams also work best on stillwaters. Because distance usually takes precedence over delicacy, extra-fast action rods, built stiff so they cast tight loops long distances, work well on lakes. But avoid them, and choose a rod that has a medium or slightly fast action, if you'll be using the same rod to fish both lakes and streams.

Reels.

The same single-action reel you use on streams will work perfectly on lakes. But stillwater trout don't burn up energy fighting a current, so they often grow larger than any trout you'll catch in a stream. So be sure that the reel you buy has room for at least 100 yards of Dacron backing line. It should also have an adequate drag system.

Leaders.

Tapered 8' to 12' leaders, the same ones you'd use on streams, are perfect for most stillwater fishing. Two situations request other leaders. If you're using a sinking line, shorten your leader to 5' or 6' feet to keep the fly from floating up above the line tip. If you're fishing a weighted nymph on a floating line, and want to get down 10' to 15', lengthen your leader to 20' or even 25', about a third of the tippet.

No matter what length leader you use, straighten it by stretching it before fishing. A leader with coils and kinks in it will have slack under the water. A trout can take your fly and move 3' or more before you feel it, or see any sign of the take. By the time you set the hook, the fish is gone.

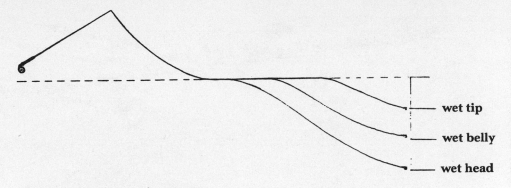

wet tip

wet belly

wet head

LINE SYSTEMS FOR LAKES

You've got to be able to explore various depths to find the level where trout hold. Two kinds of line systems allow you to do this. Choose one and build around it. Each starts with a floating line, the one you'll use most of the time.

Floating/Sinking Lines.

To fish the various depths, you can buy extra-fast sinking lines in 10' wet-tip, 20' wet-belly, and 30' wet-head. The wet-tip will let you fish from 3' to 6' down; the wet-belly will let you fish from 6' to 12' deep; the wet-head will get you down 12' to about 20' if you give it enough time to sink. Each line should be wound on a spare reel spool.

Shooting Head System.

In this system, you buy or build 30' to 40' heads the right weight to balance your rod. Use loops to fasten the heads to 100' of running line. Each head sinks at a different rate: floating, slow sinking, fast sinking, and extra-fast sinking. They can be carried coiled in a wallet, saving the space and expense of extra reel spools.

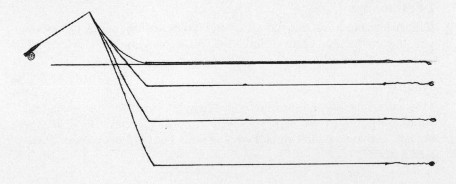

FISHING LAKES FROM SHORE

Most folks think you can't fish a lake or pond unless you've got a float tube or boat. But trout are found around the edges of lakes most of the fishing season, going deep only when the weather is very hot or very cold. They are most active, and most eager for your flies, when they're in the shallows, where you can often reach them from the bank or while wading.

Bank Fishing.

On lots of lakes, the water drops off 2' to 4' deep right at the bank. Wherever this is true, you can fish from shore as long as you have room for a backcast. Even without such room, you can reach the most productive water, right at the edge, with roll casts. Because the water is still, and the cast can disturb fish in shallow water, wait awhile before beginning your retrieve, to let things settle.

Log-Hopping.

If fallen logs probe out into the water, and if they are big enough to support you, they make great casting platforms. Walk softly, and be very careful.

Wading.

Most lakes have sloped shorelines and firm bottoms. You can wade, but watch for potholes and soft spots. When wading, always move slowly enough so that you don't spread wading waves out in front of you. These alarm trout.

AQUATIC TRANSPORTATION

Cartoppers.

Boats that fit on the roof rack of your car often work well on lakes. But recall a couple of things. A gas motor will frighten fish. It's best to anchor, row, use an electric motor, or just drift while you're fishing. And if the cartopper is aluminum, any noise you make in the boat will alarm fish in the water. Don't bang around. Use carpet to quiet it.

Prams.

A small wooden pram makes an excellent fishing platform. With a simple anchoring system, you can hover over weedbeds or park just off the shoreline. A pram is easy to row and quiet. If it's stable, you can stand to cast, an advantage for spotting fish, and for casting a long distance.

Float Tubes.

Your single best investment for stillwater fishing might be a float tube. It stores easily, can be transported in any rig, and it gives excellent access to lots of water. If you're thinking about buying a new fly rod for lakes, in order to fish them better, buy a float tube instead. It will make your old rod perform wondrously. Of course, you'll need waders and flippers for your float tube, but the waders you already own for stream fishing will do fine.

LAKE FOOD FORMS

Some of the food forms found in stillwaters are the same as those found in streams, but many are different. It's wise to make up a separate fly box especially for lake and pond fishing.

Mayfly Nymphs.

Mayfly nymphs found in stillwaters are agile swimmers. Your dressings for them should be slim, tied on long-shank hoods, and fished with brisk retrieves.

Damselfly Nymphs.

These are up to an inch long, sinuously slender. Their imitations should include soft marabou for action, and should be retrieved slowly.

Dragonfly Nymphs.

Reaching 2″ in length, these hourglass-shaped nymphs creep along, or swim in darts. Their imitations should be either crawled along the bottom, or fished with staccato strips.

Scuds.

These small crustaceans swim awkwardly around weedbeds. Fish their imitations slowly, with a hand-twist retrieve.

Midges.

The important pupal stage is tiny and hangs in the surface film. Fish its imitations shallow, with an agonizingly slow retrieve.

Leeches.

These look like night crawlers, but swim like snakes. Use Wooly Buggers to imitate them, and fish them fast at times, alternated with slow at other times, to find what the fish want.

A LAKE FLY BOX

Row 1: Adams (#12-#16), Adams Midge (#14-#18), Griffith's Gnat (#16-#10), Elk Hair Caddis (#10-#16)

Row 2: Gold Ribbed Hare's Ear (#12-#16), Prince Nymph (#10-#14), Otter Nymph (#12-#16)

Row 3: Olive Scud (#12-#16), Backswimmer (#12-#14), Midge Pupa (#14-#20), TDC (#12-#18)

Row 4: Alder Wet (#10-#14), McGinty Bee (#10-#14), Black Gnat Wet (#12-#16)

Row 5: Green Damsel (#10-#12), Carey Special (#8-#12)

Row 6: Black Wooly Bugger (#6-#12), Lead-Eye Wooly Bugger (#6-#12), Black Marabou Muddler (#6-#12)

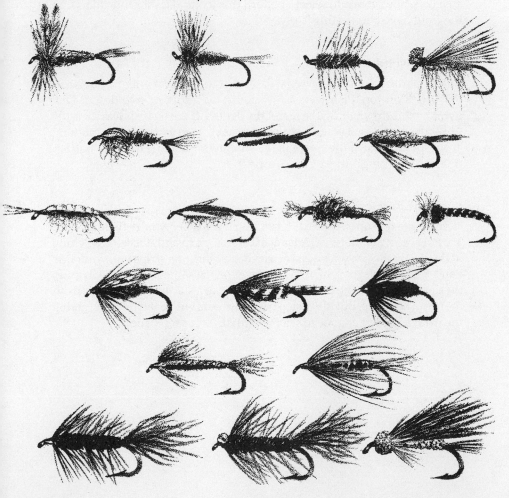

THE THREE MAJOR VARIABLES IN LAKE FLY FISHING

When fishing lakes, it can seem like you have a nightmarish number of aspects to deal with. But you're really dealing with only three major variables: the fly pattern fished, the depth at which you fish it, and the speed at which you retrieve it. Get these three right, and you've got the trout cornered.

Fly Pattern.

The first factor in fly selection is observation of any insect or other food form sitting on the surface, hovering in the air, or swimming about in the shallows. The second factor is anything you find when you take a stomach sample from a trout, or when you do some minor collecting in the shallows. Your goal is to select a pattern that looks at least a little like what the trout have been eating lately.

Depth Fished.

The fly pattern you've selected will predict the level at which you fish it. Fish dries on top. Fish wets a few inches to a foot or two down. Fish nymphs and streamers in the rest of the depths. If the water is less than 10″ to 12″ deep, try to get your sunk fly down as close as you can to the bottom. Trout spend most of their time in the shallows, but hang near the bottom unless something entices them upward.

Speed of Retrieve.

It's best to experiment with different retrieves when you're fishing lakes. Try a very slow hand-twist. Advance to a slow strip and staccato twitching of the rod tip. Finish with a fast retrieve, making long strips with your line hand. It's possible to try all three retrieves on the same cast: let the fly sink, then hand-twist it a bit, pause, then kick it up to a staccato twitch, and from there to a fast strip. But it's best to try a few casts with each retrieve, giving the trout a patient chance to see the fly fished at each pace.

DRY FLY STRATEGIES FOR LAKES

Use dry flies when you see trout cruising and feeding, or when you feel that they would be disposed to feed on the surface if they spot something, such as your fly, floating up top. Dries are excellent when you see insects in the air and on the water. They are not the best choice when the water is hot and nothing stirs, or when the lake looks cold and lifeless.

Fishing Dries to Rises.

When a trout rises in range, cast softly a couple of feet to the near side of the rise, so your line won't spook the trout. Let the fly sit a minute, then cast to one side of the rise. Let it sit, lift it again, and cast to the other side. If trout are rising all around, don't put them down by constant casting into every rise ring. Just let the fly sit.

The Searching Dry.

When no trout rise, but you feel they'll take dries, cast over shallow weedbeds, near any cover, or a foot or two out from the shoreline. Let the fly sit a minute, then pick it up and cast again to the next bit of cover.

The Skittered Dry.

Some insects scoot across the water, and trout will often take a fly that is skated over the surface. Try this with flies such as the heavily hackled Elk Hair Caddis. Just lift the rod and line to slide the fly toward you.

NYMPH STRATEGIES FOR LAKES

Most natural nymphs and larvae in lakes creep along very slowly, or else swim briskly, with darting motions. Your retrieves should mimic these two kinds of movement.

Hand-Twist Retrieve.

This is a slow rolling motion of your line hand. Catch the line with your forefinger and rotate it back toward the reel. Then catch the line with your little finger, rotate it to draw in a few more inches of line. Repeat the motion slowly, creeping the fly along. Hold your rod low, aimed right down the line.

Staccato Strip.

Drape the line over the forefinger of your rod hand, and keep the rod tip low. Draw line in with short strips: 4″ to 10″. You can add a rhythmic twitching of the rod tip to impart darts, or omit this and make the fly look like an insect swimming along in short bursts.

Countdown Method.

To fish your nymph at a specific level, count seconds while it sinks: "One thousand one, one thousand two, etc." When your fly ticks bottom or weeds on the retrieve, shorten the count on following casts. Whenever you catch a fish, repeat the count and you've achieve the same depth. It will usually take 20 to 60 seconds to get the fly down where you want it.

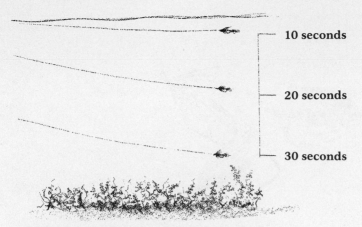

10 seconds

20 seconds

30 seconds

STREAMER STRATEGIES FOR LAKES

Countdown to Bottom or Weedbeds.

When fishing streamers in the shallows, get them down near the bottom. When fishing weedbeds, the fly should cruise along just above the weeds. Use the countdown method to get the fly deep, then vary your retrieve from a slow strip to a full gallop.

Trolling for the Thermocline.

When trout go deep to get cool in hot weather, they suspend just above the thermocline. Find one fish and you've found the depth of others. Use an extra-fast sinking line. Cast it out, let it sink a long time, then slowly troll away from it. Vary your trolling speed and the sink time until you hit a fish. Then continue fishing at that same depth

Probing the Shoreline.

Trout often hold right at the edge. Hold your float tube or pram off shore about 40'. Cast something like a black or olive Wooly Bugger tight to the bank, let it sink a few seconds, then retrieve it out with a stripping retrieve. Move along and cast to all of the bank and to any cover near it.

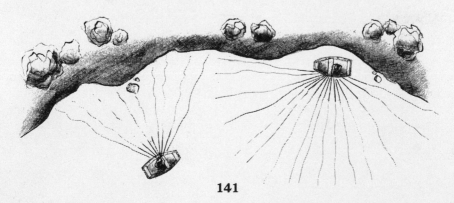

WET FLY STRATEGIES

Wet flies can be fished in all of the same ways as nymphs and streamers. In addition, they're effective when cast to rises, especially if the trout won't take a dry. Try casting a wet to a rise, then let it sink. Don't give it any action, but watch the line tip for the dart that indicates a take. If nothing happens, retrieve very slowly. Feeding trout seem to like wets on the sink, or moving at a slow idle.

Two Fly Setups.

It's often advantageous to fish two flies on the same cast, especially when you're trying to find fish. This offers the fish an option. Try a streamer at the point, with a small wet fly or nymph as the dropper. Or try two nymphs of different sizes and colors. This author's favorite combo is a #6 or #8 Olive Wooly Bugger chasing a #14 or #16 TDC.

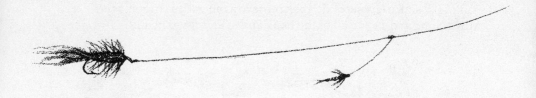

FISHING A POD OF TROUT

When you've found a pod of trout, whether they're feeding on the surface, cruising up where you can see them, or holding down deep where you can only feel for them with your fly, the biggest danger is frightening them all away after you've caught just one. Keep them calm and you might catch three or four.

When you find a pod of feeding trout, keep your tube, boat, or wadered legs as far away from them as you can cast with accuracy and delicacy: for most of us, about 35' to 45'. Move slowly; don't make waves. Cast to the near edge of the pod, so your line doesn't fly over the fish and send them fleeing.

When fishing over a cruising pod, try to determine the direction of its movement. Place yourself in a position to intercept the fish. Have your fly in place, if possible, as they approach you. Often a pod will cruise repetitively in a large circle, and you can hook a fish each time they pass.

When fishing deep, the problem is to keep in touch with a pod after you've caught one fish. It's critical to keep your fly fishing at the depth where you caught the first fish. Then criss-cross the area where you caught it, to intercept the pod.

TROLLING AND WIND DRIFTING

Trolling with Flies.

When trout are not active, you can still find them and catch them. One way to do it is simply to tie on a favorite nymph, wet fly, or streamer, or a combination of two of them. Then cast out and just idle along in a float tube or boat. It's best to troll with a wet-tip line or shooting head that gets the fly down a few feet. Work water that is 5' to 15' deep. It's rarely wise to leave the shoreline far behind and troll out in the unproductive depths of a lake.

Wind Drifting.

This method is most useful when the wind is up and the lake is rough. Use a floating line and short casts, 25' to 35'. Fish a dry fly with a wet tied 3' to 4' behind it. You can drop a weighted nymph 3' to 4' behind the wet. This setup will tangle if you try to cast it far or often. Just get it out and let the wind push you along in your tube or boat. Hold the rod high, causing the dry fly to dance. The flies below it will jump eagerly up and down. Trout will whack something.

STILLWATER TIPS

Bottom of the Shallows.

Fish spend most of the fishing season in water 3' to 12' deep. They're not always visible. If they are, fish for them where you see them, up top. Whenever they're not visible, get your fly as close to the bottom as you can. That's where trout spend most of their idle time.

Locating Weedbeds.

You can find weedbeds by trolling with your fly. If it comes up with greenery attached, you've found a good place to fish. On sunny days, when the surface is calm, you'll often see dark patches on the surface that look like the shadows of tiny clouds. Those are weedbeds down below. Fish them.

Straighten Your Leader.

Be certain to straighten your leader by stretching it, or by running it through a rubber patch; an inch square of old inner tube will do. If the leader is straight, when a fish hits you'll feel it, or see the line tip dart. If the leader is not straight, you will never know about most of the hits that you get.

Buy a Float Tube.

If you're thinking about making a single investment to improve your stillwater fly fishing, make it a float tube. A tube costs less than a new rod, and won't take up much more room to store. But a tube will give you access to an infinity of water you can't reach without one, and it will make fishing such a pleasure that you'll feel you're suspended in air.

A System for Exploring All Depths.

Settle on one line system that will let you fish all the depths of a lake. You might choose a wet-tip, wet-belly, wet-head system. An alternate is a system of full sinking lines in various sink rates. Or you can carry a wallet of shooting heads. They all work. Stick with one and concentrate on working out the mysteries of the dark depths.

Chapter 7
Fly Fishing for Bass

Bass are fiercely predaceous, eating essentially anything that is too small or too timid to eat them. They are happy to attack flies, even those that do not resemble any of nature's creatures. Fly rodders who are after bass can toss quite a range of fancies at them with some assurance of success.

Largemouth bass prefer stillwater that is warmer than that which trout can survive. Smallmouth bass live in either still or moving water. They prefer a temperature range just above that required by trout. As a consequence, smallmouth and trout populations often overlap.

Largemouth and smallmouth bass can be distinguished by a few distinct characteristics. The jaw of the largemouth extends beyond the eye, the jaw of the smallmouth to the eye. The dorsal fin of the largemouth is separated into two distinct halves; the smallmouth dorsal is continuous. The largemouth is black to dark greenish on the back, and has a band from front to back. The smallmouth is light green, brown, or bronze on the back, and has vertical stripes on its sides.

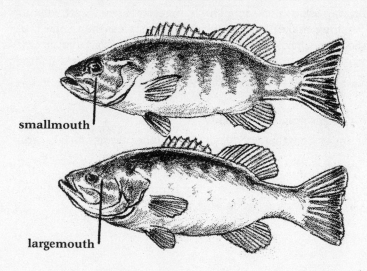

smallmouth

largemouth

LARGEMOUTH WATER TYPES

Largemouth bass are warmwater fish. Their favorite water types tend to be shallow and weedy, since shallow water warms up fastest, and with all of its sunlight, has the most plant growth. Largemouth tend to be associated with lily pads, cattails, bulrushes, and underwater growth such as elodea and eelgrass. The primary foods that sustain bass are aquatic insects, and the variety of small fishes that feed on insects. Insects thrive in weeds, so bass are happy there.

Largemouth are most comfortable in water that's about 65 to 75 degrees. They will move down into deeper water if the surface gets much warmer than that. They also do well in rather sterile habitats as long as they can find enough food to thrive. Reservoirs, for example, do not promote weed growth because water fluctuations along the shoreline keep aquatic plants from taking root. But bass do well in these waters, and can be found wherever a structure, such as a rocky point, attracts baitfish.

You'll find largemouth bass most often in ponds and lakes, but they're not strangers to backwater sloughs of streams and rivers. They will inhabit moving water, too, if the current is weak and the water is warm.

LARGEMOUTH RANGE AND DISTRIBUTION

Largemouth bass were originally native to the Mississippi River region, the Great Lakes area, the southeastern states, and Mexico. They have now been transplanted to nearly any water that will support them. Their current range is essentially the entire continental United States. They are a prime farm pond and lowland lake fish from the Pacific coast through the midwest to the New England states, and into southern Canada. Most low-altitude reservoirs have been planted with largemouth, along with the panfish and other forage fish upon which bass thrive.

Altitude is a limiting factor, because of cold water and a short growing season. Largemouth do poorly if the water temperature fails to get above 65 degrees and remain there for some weeks. So these bass are not found at all in alpine lakes, and are more a creature of the plains and the foothills than they are of any mountain ranges.

Largemouth Size.

Largemouth bass grow fastest and largest where water temperatures remain in their favored range most of the year. The record fish, weighing more than 23 pounds, was caught in Georgia more than 50 years ago. They still reach 20 pounds in Georgia and Florida, though anything over 10 pounds is a fine trophy. In the middle latitudes of their range, bass rarely exceed 8 pounds. In the northern regions, they range more commonly from 2 to 3 pounds, and a 6- to 7-pound fish is truly a trophy.

Recently, transplants of Florida strain largemouth have been introduced into rich and warm southern California reservoirs. These fish have sprung to great size. Many over 20 pounds have been taken. The 50-year-old record is put in danger each season.

BASS COVER

One thing: largemouth bass can't close their eyes. So what? Here's what: to keep the sun out of their eyes, they need to find shade if they're in shallow water. Another thing: largemouth swim fast but in brief bursts. So they must lurk around, then ambush their prey. These two things tell you a lot.

You find largemouth bass in places where they can get out of the sun, and where they can conceal an ambush. Once you've got that figured out, you know where to fish for them. Look for lily pad flats, underwater stumps, fallen trees, and the edges of reed and bulrush forests. Down a little deeper, they gather around rocky points and shoals. The depth protects their eyes from the sun, and the rocks give them hides to set ambushes.

LARGEMOUTH FOOD TYPES

Largemouth bass eat nearly anything that swims. When they are small, their major prey is aquatic insects. As they grow, their attention turns to bigger bites: the various things that live on those same aquatic insects. This includes schooling panfish such as bluegill, crappie, and perch. Bass enjoy frogs, salamanders, and even snakes that make the mistake of taking to water. Mice and shrews often fall in along the edges, scramble, and cause detonations. They're among the reasons that your poppers and hair bugs can cause the same kinds of explosions. But the simple aggression of the bass—their willingness to try anything that doesn't try them—is what makes them such a fine fly rod quarry.

Cork Poppers.

These creations resemble frogs or beetles or figments of our own imaginations. They range from small ones tied on #6 and #8 hooks to giants tied on #2/0 hooks. It's critical that you have them in a range of colors, say, black, white, yellow, green, plus red and white together. Bass are often fussy about color; if your first choice doesn't work after 20 minutes or so, switch.

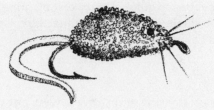

Hair Bugs.

These are tied with deer hair spun on the hook, then clipped. They usually have some slight resemblance to a frog or a mouse. They are extremely effective, landing on the water gently. They are soft, so bass hold onto them a bit longer than cork poppers before spitting them out. Hair bugs come in the same range of sizes as poppers.

Streamers.

Regular trout streamers work for bass, especially the brightest of Wooly Buggers and Marabou Muddlers. Most streamers tied especially for bass, such as Dave Whitlock's Eelworm Streamer, are long and look like slithering snakes or prowling salamanders.

TACKLE FOR LARGEMOUTH BASS

Rods.

Because the poppers, bugs, and streamers you'll cast for largemouth bass are large and wind-resistant, rods for them should handle 7- to 9-weight lines. But if your heaviest rod at the moment is a 6-weight, you can easily arm it with a weight-forward 7-weight line and restrict yourself to the smaller sizes in the bass fly categories. The bass will be happy; so will you. The rod should be 8½' to 9½' long, with a moderate to slightly fast taper.

Reels.

Your reel must hold the line you'll be using. That's all. You don't need backing. You won't play largemouth bass off the drag as you do trout, because they tire too quickly to make long runs. The reel you have, or an inexpensive single-action if you must buy one, will do for all your largemouth fishing needs.

Lines.

Double-taper floating lines work well enough with the smallest largemouth flies. Weight-forward tapers are better because you'll be after distance a lot more often than delicacy. Special bass bug tapers are weight-forward lines with most of the casting weight stacked right behind a short front taper. Get one if you plan to cast the heaviest largemouth poppers and bugs. Add an extra-fast sinking wet-tip line, in weight-forward taper, for fishing streamers, and you've got all the lines that you need.

Leaders.

Leaders for largemouth should be about 6' to 8' long, and need not be tapered. Use a level stretch of 10# to 15# monofilament. Knotless leaders are important: in weedy bass cover, knots constantly get hung up on lily pads, or gather strings of weeds, spooking the bass and hindering your fishing. For fishing deep with streamers, keep your level leader to about 4' to 5' long, so the fly doesn't ride up above the bottom, where the sink-tip line has delivered it.

FLOAT TUBES AND PRAMS

When bass fishing on ponds and small lakes, if you find some way to get out onto the water, you will have an enormous advantage. The reason is simple: most bass cover forms along the edges of a lake or pond, and you can catch a lot more fish if you can get out and cast back toward it.

Float Tubes.

Because bass water is often small, remote, and somewhat swampy, a float tube is ideally suited not only for getting to the water, but also getting around on it. Also, a tube is nearly silent, and you move around with very little disturbance. Bass fishing is similar to trout fishing in lakes: if you're going to make a single wise investment to improve your fishing, it should be a float tube.

Prams.

Nothing can beat the simple pleasure of paddling a pram around on a foggy dawn, probing pad flats, stumps, and fallen logs for lurking bass. Wooden prams are quiet; they are stable platforms for standing up and casting; they are swift to row from place to place. If a pram has a single advantage over a float tube, it is the increase in range you've got: you can row about five times faster than you can paddle. Add a simple anchoring system, so you can hold your position in a wind, and you're set.

CARTOPPERS AND BASS BOATS

If you intend to fish bigger water, such as a large lake or reservoir, then you'll find that good bass cover is scattered. You'll need some sort of motor-propelled transportation.

Cartoppers.

A 10' to 12' aluminum boat makes a fine casting platform. Do all you can to silence the oars, and put a throw-rug under your feet to keep them from banging the boat. An electric trolling motor allows a silent approach that you can rarely achieve with aluminum and oars.

Bass Boats.

The ultimate for bass fishing, on big water, comes in the form of a fancy bass boat, rigged with elevated swivel seats and carpeted casting platforms. A fire-breathing motor rushes you between widely separated pieces of bass cover; an electric motor tugs you along silently while you fish them.

TIME OF SEASON, TIME OF DAY

Largemouth bass are sensitive to sun and to water temperature. Their movements up and down in the depths and their activities during each day are highly dependent upon what the day brings. Of course when food is active bass are also active, no matter what the other factors might predict.

Time of Season.

Largemouth bass move into the shallows as soon as the water warms in spring. They are warmwater fish, so they respond quickly to the heat of the sun. Bass prefer water from 65 to 75 degrees, but they move up as soon as the water is warmer on top than it is on the bottom. That means they'll be up as early as March or April, when the water is still around 50 degrees.

In summer, when the surface water gets too warm, largemouth bass move down to cooler depths, and you've got to probe for them with your wet-tip or even full sinking lines. In fall, they move briefly into the shallows again. In winter, largemouth bass go deep and lie nearly dormant. It's a tough time to fish for them with flies.

Time of Day.

Because largemouth bass cannot close their eyes to shut out the sun, they are shallowest and most active at dawn and dusk, when the sun does not strike the water. No matter what season, the best times to pursue largemouth with a fly rod are in the first two hours of daylight, and again in the last two hours of daylight. Along the same lines, you'll do far better fishing for bass all day if it's cloudy than you will if it's bright.

FISHING TOPWATER COVER

Largemouth bass are most fun when taken on top, where you can see the explosion. Before making your cast, recall that the senses of the bass— sight and hearing—are its main line of defense, and also provide its main impulse to attack. You've got to present your lure as prey, not as a predator.

The Topwater Twitch.

Cast your popper or bug softly, 1' to 3' from cover. Let it sit for 30 to 60 seconds, but keep your eyes on it. Often largemouth slip up and sip a fly with little disturbance. If there is no take, tighten the line and twitch the lure, then let it sit again. Repeat this four or five times. Finally, retrieve with twitches and pauses for about 10' out from the cover before lifting the lure and casting again.

The Topwater Pop.

Sometimes bass will refuse your topwater lure unless you make noise with it. If the topwater twitch fails, try jerking the lure to make it gurgle and pop and splash.

Lily Pads.

Make your first cast to the outside edge of a pad flat. Let the fly sit, then retrieve with the topwater twitch. Make following casts back into pockets in the pads. Again, let the fly sit, then just twitch it, because the retrieve will disturb the water as soon as your fly tangles with pads. That first twitch is the most likely to incite a strike.

Stumps.

Make your first cast short of a stump by 3' to 4', to avoid frightening bass holding under it. Make the next cast right to the stump. Then place casts beyond the stump on either side, retrieving the fly back past it.

Logs.

Approach a submerged log from the side, and cast straight into it. Move around it slowly, fishing all possible lies from both sides. Make your final cast parallel to the length of the log. If your first cast does this, your line might frighten fish all along the length of the log. Even if it doesn't, you've fished out most of the lies with only one marginal cast.

Shorelines.

Bass often hang all along a shoreline, especially if it is rocky, or has overhanging brush. Cover every bit of it. Three feet is too far out; cast right onto the shore. If your topwater fly is weedless, you can cast onto land and walk it off and into the water. Fish each cast out about 10', then pick the fly up and place the next cast about 3' to 4' down the shoreline from the one before it.

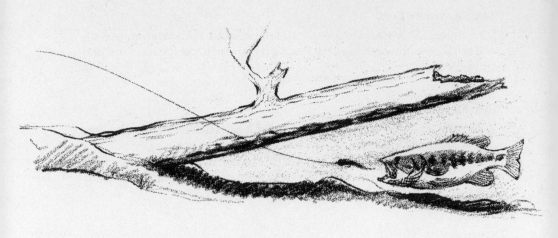

FISHING UNDERWATER FLIES

Bass are often shy about taking on top when the sun is bright. If the fish are on the bottom in water that is more than about 6' deep, they'll also be difficult to move to the top. If the water is colder than 60 degrees, they'll be a bit sluggish, and you might need to put a fly in front of their noses before they'll take it. These are excellent times to fish streamers.

The Bottom Slide.

Bass usually find their food on the bottom creeping along. That's the way you should retrieve streamers down deep: with the very slowest retrieve you can manage.

The Mid-Water Strip.

When fishing a streamer that resembles a minnow, swim it along like the real thing. Fish it from just under the surface to about 10' down. Once it's sunk to the depth you want it, then bring it back in fast strips. Make it look like a small fish trying to escape a bass hot on its tail.

Fishing Pad Flats.

Fish a streamer through a pad flat by casting it far back in among the pads, then crawling it out. Let it climb up onto a pad, slide across, and settle back into the water. Watch your line tip; takes are always very subtle.

Submerged Logs.

Fish these as you would with a topwater lure, from the sides, casting straight in among the limbs. Make sure your streamer has a weedguard. Land it right above the submerged log, then let it settle slowly down alongside it. Once it has reached the bottom, slide it out very slowly. Watch your line tip; you'll rarely feel the inhalation of your lure.

Rocky Points.

Fish points with heavily weighted streamers. Cast near shore, and let the lure settle to the bottom. Retrieve slowly; allow the streamer to bounce down from level to level as you fish it away from shore. It often helps to cast across the point from the side, and crawl the fly up onto the point.

Weedbeds.

To fish a submerged weedbed with a streamer, use a weighted fly and a fast-sinking wet-tip line. Cast out and count the fly down to the weeds. Then retrieve slowly right through them. If weeds gather on the streamer, shorten the count to fish it right above them.

Weedguards.

Because of the wicked cover where you'll fish streamers, it's almost mandatory to have weedguards. If you buy your flies, insist on this. If you tie your own, bind 25# monofilament at the bend of the hook. When you've finished tying the rest of the fly, bring the mono up under the eye and wrap it down, to protect the hook point.

HOOKING AND PLAYING BASS

Detecting a take is no problem when you fish topwater lures, though at times the fish will slip up and sip them while you're napping. Most often, though, they bust them, and the take is quite obvious, even if you're asleep. Set the hook as soon as you see the take; bass won't hold onto a fly for long.

With underwater lures, especially those fished slowly, detecting a take is far more difficult. You'll probably only notice about one-third of the takes that you get. So it's absolutely necessary to be wide awake and watchful. Focus on your line tip, or the spot where the line or leader enters the water. If it twitches, rear back hard to set the hook. Often the take will be signaled by a sideways movement of the line tip or leader. Again, set the hook quickly and hard. Bass have hard mouths. If you set the hook as gently as you do on trout, you will lose most of them.

Playing Bass.

Once you've got the hook set, get the bass moving your way as quickly as you can, and keep it coming. Bass rarely make strong runs, taking line off the reel. You play them by hand, drawing line in with the line hand while controlling the fish by holding the line tight with the rod hand forefinger. Strip line hard; there's little chance you'll pull the hook out of the mouth of a bass once it's been hooked.

The Flap and the Dash.

Bass are rather violent fish, and they're played the way they live. They flap in the air and dash about, and you draw them toward your hand while they're still fresh and full of fight. It's best to land them this way, so you can release them while they're still strong. Playing a bass is a different kind of excitement than playing a trout: it all happens in a hectic hurry.

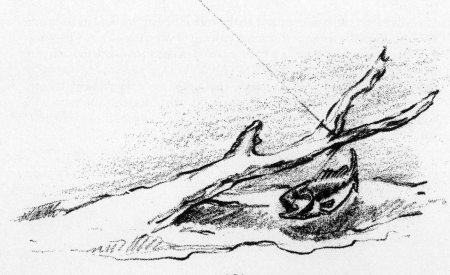

LANDING BASS

The best way to subdue a bass is to lip it. If you did this to trout, you'd break their lower jaws, thereby killing them. But bass are notoriously hardy, and lipping them does not harm them if you're gentle. Of course, they can be netted, too, the same way as trout: get their heads up and lead them over the rim of the net. Never try to stab at them with the net. You'll only knock them off.

To lip a bass, first subdue it with the rod until you can hold its head out of water. If it's still thrashing around, you might wind up with the fish gone and the hook in your thumb, which is always a surprise. Once the fish can be held reasonably still, lift its head high with the rod while you reach down with your line hand. Grasp the fish by the lower jaw and lift it at an angle so the jaw hinges open. If you let it hang straight, the bass will continue to flip in your hand. Holding it at an angle causes the bass to hold still.

Remove the hook quickly, admire the fish for an instant, then lower it to the water and let it swim away. Don't pitch it in, but set it into the water gently.

LARGEMOUTH TIPS

Variety.

Largemouth bass, for some reason, are notoriously fickle. One day they'll take nothing but yellow, the next nothing but black. One day they'll be frightened by a loud retrieve, the next they'll refuse a quiet one. One day they'll bust to the top, the next they'll feed only on the bottom. So keep switching flies and tactics until you find what suits their mood of the moment.

Weedguards.

Because so much bass cover is a tangle, it's wise to have weedguards on all but a few of your topwater poppers and bugs. The bass has such a hard mouth that the guard won't cost you many fish; if you don't use guards you'll lose lots of flies.

Dawn and Dusk.

It's vital to fish when the day is cool and the light is not bright. That means before the sun rises and after it sets. On cloudy days you'll do fine all day. Otherwise, the misty times are the most pleasant and lonely to be out anyway.

The Senses of Bass.

Sight and hearing serve the bass to locate its prey, but also to keep from becoming prey. Make as little underwater noise as you can. Never bang the boat, run the motor near cover, or use squeaky oars. Be careful of your float tube waves. If you send waves over the cover ahead of you, you'll catch few fish, and you'll wonder why.

Catch and Release.

Bass are prolific spawners, but it takes them a long time to grow to good size. If you feel the need to fillet a few for the pan, take small ones, from a half pound to a pound and let the larger and older fish go. You'll get a combination of the best eating and the best fishing this way.

SMALLMOUTH BASS

Smallmouth bass survive well in water types and temperatures that bridge the gap between those preferred by largemouth and those required by trout. These brisker bass are native to flowing water; they are often found in warmwater streams that are too fast for largemouth, but that also reach the 80-degree temperature limit that is fatal to trout.

Smallmouth are also found in lakes that are too cold for largemouth happiness, but again that approach or exceed summer temperatures marginal for trout. As a consequence, smallmouth thrive in a wide range of waters that are at best marginal for either largemouth bass or trout.

If water temperatures in a lake or pond get high enough for largemouth bass for a substantial part of the year, then smallmouth territories will overlap with those bucketmouth bass. If temperatures in a lake or stream remain low enough to keep from killing trout, then smallmouth territories will overlap with that sleeker set of species.

Because smallmouth are adapted to cooler and more often moving water, they are much stronger than largemouth. Many consider them, pound for pound, much stronger than trout.

SMALLMOUTH RANGE AND DISTRIBUTION

The original range of smallmouth bass takes in all warmwater streams and most lowland lakes in the East, Southeast, and Midwest. Perhaps their best-known native habitats are the gentle warmwater streams of the Mississippi Basin, and the lakes and reservoirs of the New England states. But smallmouth have justified their reputation as pound-for-pound the gamest of any freshwater fish, and they've been transplanted nearly everywhere that's favorable to their survival. They can now be found in nearly the entire tier of northern states, and along the southern range of the Canadian provinces.

Many streams in the arid West, where flows are gentle and where midsummer water temperatures briefly exceed those that trout can survive, have now received thriving populations of smallmouth. The typical picture of smallmouth fishing is an idle drift in a johnboat beneath streamside canopies of southern hardwoods, or paddling a canoe around the rocky edges of a northern lake. But just as often today, the picture flicks to a drift boat passing through a desert landscape of juniper trees and sagebrush.

As with largemouth, altitude and consequent cold temperatures are a limiting factor to smallmouth distribution. They are not found in the northern Rockies, in the Cascades, in the High Sierra. But their populations extend into the foothills of nearly all mountain ranges.

Smallmouth bass grow largest in the southern extent of their range, where the season for growth is longest. An 8-pound fish is a rare large one; those in the 5-# to 6-pound range are more common. In the cooler water of the middle part of the smallmouth's range, a 4-# to 5-pound fish would be an exceptional trophy. In the northern tier of states and provinces smallmouth average 1 to 2 pounds and a 4-pound fish is a very large one.

SMALLMOUTH STRUCTURE IN LAKES

Lakes that smallmouth prefer are colder than those inhabited by largemouth, and consequently have less vegetative growth. The water tends to be clean, clear, and cold in spring and fall, though it might exceed 80 degrees in mid-summer.

Because cold and clear lakes offer scant cover in the form of lily pads, cattails, and bulrushes, smallmouth bass tend to be found more often around rocks. They like tumbles of rock that drop off from shore. If the water drops off steeply, they will be close to the bank. If it steps out more gently, look for them from 10' to 50' from the shoreline itself. They are also found off any bit of shoreline that offers them some other sort of shelter.

Smallmouth bass are temperature sensitive. They move quickly to the depth that gives them what they want at the moment, which varies from 65 to 75 degrees. They often school in a stratified layer. Once you've found one fish, you're likely to find others at the same depth.

SMALLMOUTH LIES IN STREAMS

Smallmouth streams are more like trout streams than they are like the sluggish backwaters and sloughs preferred by largemouth bass. Their water has trout stream features: riffles, runs, pools, and flats. But smallmouth are found in slightly different water than the places where you would find trout.

Three things define ideal lies for smallmouth: depth, darkness, and cover. If you find a tumble of rock along the edge of a deep pool that has a slow to modest current, you've got it all. But smallmouth also hang along any edge that is fairly deep and broken by rocks or by shoreline vegetative growth. They'll gather over boulders out in med-depths. Logs fallen into the stream are favorite lies. If the bottom is seamed with ledges and trenches, bass will be found in scattered depressions.

Though smallmouth do not hold continually in riffles or fast runs, they'll move into such water whenever some food form tempts them there. Unlike largemouth, and just like trout, smallmouth respond to a hatch of mayflies or caddis, and sometimes even feed on them selectively.

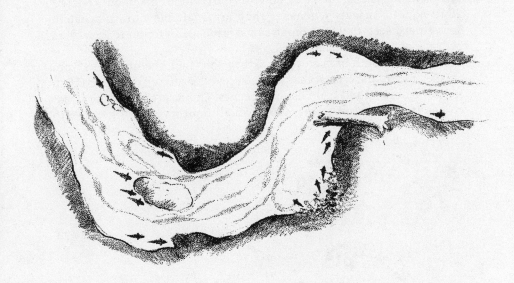

167

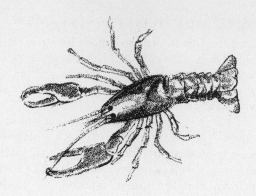

SMALLMOUTH FOODS

Smallmouth, despite their name, are equipped to take the largest bites their environment might offer. They are aggressive feeders, and will try anything as long as it looks alive and enticing. Their primary food forms include aquatic insects, crayfish and other crustaceans, and baitfish.

Mayflies, caddisflies, and hellgrammites are taken at all seasons in their nymphal and larval stages, down on the bottom. Smallmouth feed on adult aquatic insects whenever they are available during a hatch. Terrestrial insects that fall from streamside foliage, or topple to the waters of a lake, are also taken hastily.

As smallmouth bass grow large, they shift their feeding focus from smaller insects and crustaceans to the larger bites offered by such baitfish species as shiners and sculpins, plus leeches. This desire for nutrition that comes in condensed doses makes smallmouth very vulnerable to streamers.

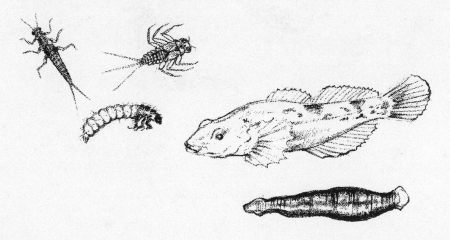

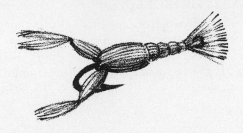

SMALLMOUTH FLY TYPES

Poppers, hair bugs, and streamers that work for largemouth bass work just as well on smallmouth. At times, though, they're more easily fooled with flies that resemble the food forms they prefer. Often they'll take the same dry flies used for trout. Crayfish flies are always effective for smallmouth bass. You should get them down and scoot them along the bottom, where the omnivorous naturals prowl.

The same nymphs that take trout will also fool smallmouth. Use nymphs tied on #4 through #10 hooks. Tumble them right down on the bottom. Pattern is probably not nearly as important as the right depth and presentation.

Most streamers that work for trout or largemouth bass will work as well for smallmouth. A few favorites include black or olive Wooly Buggers, the Black Marabou Muddler, and the Muddler Minnow.

SMALLMOUTH TACKLE

There is no need to rush out and buy anything special for smallmouth. If you've got a medium outfit, it will be perfect. If you've opted for a light, use a weight-forward line with small poppers, hair bugs, nymphs, and streamers. If you've got only a heavy, then it's more than you'll need, but it will work fine.

Rods.

The ideal smallmouth rod might be 8½' to 9' long with a moderate action, balanced to a 6-weight line. Arm it with a weight-forward 7-weight; most rods take a weight-forward one size heavier than the double-taper for which they're rated.

Reels.

Any reel you own will work for smallmouth. They do make strong runs, unlike largemouth, so a single-action reel is preferred over an automatic. But the reel need not have a fine-tuned drag system, since you'll not need to protect the fine tippets often used in trout fishing.

Lines.

The prime line for smallmouth should be a standard weight-forward floater, to balance the rod you'll be fishing. Back it up with 50 to 100 yards of braided backing line. You should also have an extra-fast sinking wet-tip line, and later might want to add a wet-belly or wet-head line in the same sink rate, to get nymphs and streamers down deep in pools or in lakes.

Leaders.

Smallmouth bass are not often leader shy. Your leader tippet can be somewhat stout, and should always be in the right range to turn over the size fly that you're casting. You'll usually be using 1X to 3X, testing out around 6# to 12#. But with smaller dry flies and nymphs, go to 4X and even 5X tippets. Leaders should be tapered, and about the length of the rod.

TIME OF SEASON, TIME OF DAY

Time of Season.

Smallmouth bass movements in lakes are not unlike those of largemouth bass or trout. As soon as shallows begin to heat up in spring, they move out of winter depths to enjoy the warmth and the sudden activity of all their favorite food forms. Spring is the banner season to fish for smallmouth in lakes, because flies are easiest to fish in shallow water.

As the water warms above 70 degrees in summer, smallmouth begin to drop back into the cooler depths. You can follow their movements with sinking lines as they drop down to 10′, then 15′, and finally below 20′. In fall, smallmouth move briefly back into shallows, as they do in spring. But they creep into their winter retreats when the days begin to chill. Then they're nearly impossible to find and entice with flies.

Time of Day.

Smallmouth bass, like largemouth, have no eyelids and do not like bright sunlight. They are usually shallow and most active in the earliest and latest hours of any given day. If the day remains cloudy, they will stay up longer. Briefly in very early spring and again in fall, smallmouth enjoy the new warmth of the sun, and are apt to be most active in the warmest part of the day: early to mid-afternoon.

Smallmouth in Streams.

Smallmouth tend to follow the same seasonal and daily cycles in streams that they do in lakes. But they do not have the depths for retreat, so they retreat into inactivity. Any food that is available will coax them out of it at almost any season, and any time of day. But they are most available and most active in spring, summer, and early fall, least active in winter. When the weather is hot and the sun beats down, smallmouth in streams are best fished for at dawn and at dusk, just as in lakes. When the weather is cool, they will feed all day.

FLY FISHING FOR SMALLMOUTH BASS IN LAKES

Wading.

When fishing from shore, it's a natural tendency to cast straight out into the lake, but don't limit yourself to that. Instead, pick a position and cast along the shoreline to one side, than fan your casts in an arc until you're casting straight out. Finish by working the arc around until you're fishing along the shoreline on your other side. Poke the fly into any pockets you can reach.

Float Tube or Boat.

Most of your casts for smallmouth bass should be made from out in the water, back in toward the bank. Stalk as quietly as you can. Don't bang the boat. Don't rock the tube and send waves ahead over the water you want to fish.

Fishing the Surface.

In spring and early summer, begin fishing with a floating line. Use a popper or hair bug. Cast right to the shore, and fish carefully around any obvious cover: overhanging brush, a fallen log, or lily pad flats. Cast carefully to rocky shorelines and rocky points. They're favorite smallmouth hangouts. Use the topwater twitch, fishing the lure very patiently and quietly. Smallmouth are more bashful than largemouth. If surface lures don't work, stick with the floating line, but switch to a streamer. Fish it slowly at the edges of cover and down rocky points.

Fishing the Depths.

In mid-summer and afterward, you'll probably need to go deeper to find the fish. Rig up with an extra-fast sinking wet-head line and a weighted streamer or crayfish fly. Cast straight in toward the shoreline. Let the fly settle to the bottom, then begin retrieving it out slowly, walking it down the bottom as deep as it will go. Bass are usually at one restricted level down there; they're also usually near the bottom, not suspended out in open water. So a lure that hikes down the sloped bottom will be spotted by them at one time or another.

It's important to cover lots of shoreline in this type of fishing, because smallmouth tend to school up. Once you've caught one, stay in the same place and fish it thoroughly. If you don't catch any more there, look for similar cover or shorelines elsewhere in the lake, and fish them just as carefully.

Movement.

In fishing for smallmouth bass on still waters, movement is very important. You've got to keep going until you find the fish, because the fish are not going to come to you.

FLY FISHING FOR SMALLMOUTH IN RIVERS AND STREAMS

Cycles.

Smallmouth in rivers and streams move up onto the banks, or to shallow riffles and runs, in spring and early summer, then down to deeper runs and pools in mid-summer. They return to the shallows briefly in fall, then return to the depths for winter.

Holding Water.

Look for a feature that indicates a good holding lie. It might be a bouldery bank that drops off into water at least 2′ to 4′ deep. Ledges and deep trenches in a bedrock bottom always attract smallmouth. Mid-water boulders tend to gather a few fish. Deep runs have invisible holding lies on the bottom, as do deep pools. Tailouts of pools often hold smallmouth whenever some food form is active there.

Fishing From Shore.

If you can't get out from shore, then fish from the bank itself. Make your casts quartering out and across the current, about 20′ to 30′ from the bank. Then swim the fly in toward shore. This works best with streamers, but you can also slide a hair bug or popper over the surface. Fish each cast to the bank, then move down a couple of steps and cast again.

Fishing Banks.

The best way to fish a bank is to wade out, then cast back right to it with a popper, hair bug, or streamer. Let the fly float or sink for a moment, then retrieve it out with twitches and short strips. Cover the water with just a cast or two, and move on. Be careful to cover any obvious features.

Wading.

Wade out and fish trenches and ledges with poppers or streamers retrieved right above them or through them. Fish runs and tailouts with large weighted nymphs and streamers. Use sinking lines to get them to the bottom. Cast across stream, and fish the flies down and around. You can also fish nymphs upstream, with indicator and split shot, just as you would for trout. It's often effective to swim a streamer across the lip of a tailout. You'll sometimes see the thin water wellup just before a bass detonates on your fly.

Floating.

If you're floating a stream in a canoe, johnboat, or drift boat, it's best to pop your fly right to the shoreline. Retrieve it out just 10' or so, then lift it for the next cast. Keep your eye out for any mid-water feature worth a cast or two.

SMALLMOUTH TIPS

Canoeing.

Most smallmouth lakes and streams are perfect for the graceful and silent canoe. On lakes, it pays to have some sort of anchor to hold your position. On streams, it's best to part the canoe and wade when you reach likely looking water, though you can also idle along and cast as you go.

Pounding the Banks.

If you've got a pram or a small drift boat that lets you stand up and cast, floating along on a river or even rowing along the edges of a lake while casting to every bit of bank, is an extremely effective way to catch some smallmouth bass and also to see some beautiful country. One person should row while one or two others stand and fish. Switch off.

Fighting Smallmouth.

Smallmouth are far stronger than largemouth, and have the endurance to make runs like trout. A 2-# to 4-pound fish puts up a violent fight, with lots of jumps and long runs. Be patient when one is hooked. You won't be able to lead it right in and lip it, though that is still the best way to land one once it's defeated.

No Need for New Gear.

Almost everybody lives within striking range of smallmouth water, but not everybody takes the time to try for them. It's too bad, because they're wonderful fish, and it takes no new gear to fish for them. Just trot out your trout rods and reels, and take along your largemouth lures. That's all. You can gear up more specifically later, if you need to.

Once Hooked, Always Hooked.

Until you've battled a scrappy smallmouth, it's hard to describe what is so exciting about fishing for them. They dash out of cover, strike violently like largemouth, then fight a battle that exceeds their size. Once you've hooked your first one, you'll always be hooked on smallmouth bass.

Chapter 8
Fly Fishing for Panfish

Panfish are named for their convenient fit in a frying pan, an for the delight they provide once they get there. But the primary delight to be derived from these feisty little fish is their willingness to take a fly, and the dogged fight they put up once they're hooked. Because most species have small mouths, and therefore feed on small insects and crustaceans, they are best duped with the size lures that are easily cast with fly rods. They're perfect fly rod fish.

All panfish congregate in schools, and most panfish species are prolific spawners. It's common for them to overpopulate a body of water and become stunted. You will help the overall fish population by frying a few. This will increase the average size of those left, and thereby improve your own fishing.

PANFISH SPECIES

The bluegill is the most popular panfish. It is built like the shape of your hand when held flat. They range up to a maximum 15″, and just over 4 pounds. But a ½ to 1½ pound specimen will put up a fine fight. Several related sunfish species, also called *bream* or *brim,* are similar in size, appearance, and habits to the bluegill. These include redear and pumpkinseed.

Black crappie and white crappie are nearly alike, separated by the slightly increased dark spotting of the black. Their habits are similar, though the black prefers clear water, while the white prefers cloudy water. Often their schools are intermixed. Schools tend to run to a single size; a pan-sized crappie just under 1 pound is typical. Catch a ½-pound fish and the rest in that area will be of nearly the same size. Catch a 2-pound fish, and others will be like it. Crappie above that size are often loners, not found in schools.

PANFISH RANGE AND DISTRIBUTION

Bluegill originally ranged from Minnesota and the Great Lakes region south to Arkansas and Georgia. But they've since been transplanted to nearly every warmwater environment. They are common in farm ponds and lowland lakes throughout the East, Midwest, and West. Other sunfish species have been transplanted less widely; they are found most often in the southern states.

The bluegill habitat is primarily ponds and small lakes. Scattered populations are also found in reservoirs, in backwaters and sloughs, and in very slow-flowing rivers. They do not adapt well to currents, and are not found in fast streams.

Crappie originally ranged throughout the eastern states up to southern Manitoba. They have now been introduced to nearly every farm pond and low-elevation lake in the United States and the southern tier of the Canadian provinces. They are prolific in large impoundments, where black crappie enjoy the clear water and rocky structure that attracts clouds of baitfish. White crappie, conversely, are creatures of brush piles and stickups. But the habitat requirements of all panfish species are not strict. Their populations often overlap, and also overlap with those of trout and bass.

Bluegill populations tend to be steady, although they often move toward becoming overpopulated and stunted a few years after their introduction unless they're kept cropped by fishing. Crappie populations move through cycles, regardless of fishing pressure. For two to three seasons, they'll be prolific and often large. For the next two to three seasons, they'll be scattered and generally smaller. Then a new year class will take hold and thrive, and the cycle will repeat itself.

SEASONS OF THE PANFISH

Understanding the seasons can help you know where to find panfish, and at what level you'll most likely catch them. They are most available to the fly rodder when they're in shallow water. They're also the most fun when taken on topwater lures.

Spring.

This is the prime season for panfish. They'll be on and around cover associated with the shoreline: fallen trees, brush piles, lily pad flats, reed and rush edges. They'll usually be found in water 2' to 6' deep.

Summer.

As the water warms to just under 70 degrees, bluegill and crappie spawn in the shallows. Then as the water gets warmer they begin to back down to deeper and cooler water. Bluegill will hold at 8' to 15', but crappie will drop all the way to the thermocline at around 20', and stratify just above it.

Fall.

For a brief period as the water cools, both bluegill and crappie move up into water 5' to 10' deep. But as soon as the chill sets in, they'll drop back down again.

Winter.

Panfish are not very active in winter except where the water remains relatively warm: above 60 degrees. Most often, they drop down 15' to 30' and sort of hunker. It's tough to fish for them with flies then.

Latitude.

The farther south you find them in their range, the longer each season panfish will be available for fishing with flies. In the southern tier of states, fishing for them never stops. In the northern tier, the best fishing might last for just two to three months. Then they drop out of sight and become difficult to find.

PANFISH COVER IN PONDS AND LAKES

When gazing at water and wondering where to find panfish, always ask: Where can they hide, and where can they find food while they hide? Because most of their living is made eating aquatic insects, and most aquatic insects are associated with vegetative growth, panfish can be found most of the time around lily pads, reed and rush edges, and submerged weedbeds. Crappie are fond of brush piles. Wherever you find a tree toppled into the water, especially if it still owns a tangle of limbs, you're likely to find a school. Reservoirs with submerged forests or stickups are magnets to crappie. But crappie also school in clear lakes and reservoirs, where they feed on minnows. So, they are often found around rocky banks and points, on the same cover where you'll find smallmouth and largemouth bass.

Bluegill can be found in all of the same kinds of places. Overhanging brush at the edge of a lake or pond is also a favorite hangout for bluegill, especially in spring when the water is warmest in the shallows.

PANFISH WATER IN STREAMS

Panfish prefer very slow to still water, so you won't find them where the current is any more than sluggish. If there's a key to finding panfish in streams and rivers, it's to look for places where the water could be considered *ponded:* deep and nearly still. If you find some sort of cover there, then the odds are vastly increased.

Because most cover is associated with the banks in streams, look for schools of panfish along the edges. They'll be in eddies and along undercut banks, especially those with root systems of bankside trees extending beneath the water. Find a place where a tree has toppled to deep water, and you've found the prime spot.

Panfish in sluggish streams and rivers will most often be found where the water is 3′ to 8′ deep, rarely where it is only foot or so deep. But given shallow water, and some overhanging brush or cover growing up out of the water, you'll sometimes find panfish in water that's only inches deep. They're most vulnerable to the fly rodder in 2′ to 6′ of water, because it's easiest to fish a fly at those depths.

PANFISH FLIES

If you're fishing for trout and bass, you've already got most of the flies that you'll need for panfish.

Poppers and Hair Bugs.

Cork poppers and hair bugs work as well for panfish as they do for bass. Use the smallest you can find.

Sponge Spiders.

Spiders quiver as if alive, and feel soft when ingested by a bluegill or crappie. They can be kept dry and fished on the surface, or soaked to fish a few inches deep.

Nymphs.

Any trout nymph can be effective for panfish. Try standards such as the Muskrat, Gold Ribbed Hare's Ear, or Zug Bug in sizes #12 to #14.

Streamers.

Crappie feed heavily on minnows. They will take streamers readily. Try such dressings as the Mickey Finn, Muddler, or even black or olive Wooly Buggers, all in sizes #6-#10.

PANFISH TACKLE

Don't go out and buy anything special to fly fish for panfish. Use what you've already got for trout or bass. Later, if you'd like to get a light outfit exactly for panfish, this is how it should look.

Rods.

The right rod for these small fish should handle a light line and small flies, and protect delicate tippets. It should also take a deep bend at the insistence of fish that are feisty, but not dangerous. The ideal rod is 8½' to 9' long, and casts a 4-weight line. It's no surprise that this is also the perfect light rod for trout.

Reels.

You'll have no need for backing or a stern drag, so you can get by with the smallest and cheapest reel that will hold the line you choose. But it might be wise to buy a reel that will hold some backing, and that has a good drag. Then it can become the perfect light reel for trout fishing.

Lines.

For fishing the surface and the first few feet beneath it, use either a weight-forward or double-taper floater. This will be your prime line. Add a weight-forward wet-tip line in fast or extra-fast sinking, for exploring the minor depths. That's all the lines you need for panfish.

Leaders.

Panfish are not leader shy. Use the right size tippet to turn over the fly you're using (refer to chart on page 19). Level leaders will work fine, as they do for bass poppers and hair bugs. But tapered leaders will give you more accurate and delicate casts. Choose the kind without knots, and you won't gather vegetation on every retrieve. The overall length of the leader should be about the length of the rod.

PANFISH PRESENTATION

Slow describes the best retrieve for almost any fly you choose for panfish. They are very deliberate feeders, often examining a fly for a long time before finally accepting it.

When fishing poppers or hair bugs on top, use the topwater twitch. Drop the fly lightly to the water. Let it sit as much as a minute or more. Don't gaze at the scenery while it idles; panfish often sip it in with little disturbance on the surface. If nothing takes it on the sit, retrieve with slow twitches interspersed with lots of pauses.

When fishing nymphs, use the hand-twist retrieve described for stillwater trout. Give the fly some time to sink, then bring it in at a crawl. Keep a close eye on your line tip, or on the point where the leader enters the water. Your only indication of a take will be the tiniest movement.

Streamers are at times an exception to the slow rule, though most of the time it's best to inch them along through a school of fish. But when crappie attack a school of minnows, cast the fly out, let it get a few inches deep, and retrieve it back at the pace that a panicked minnow might swim.

PANFISH ON THE STRINGER

Panfish didn't get their name by accident. They are the right fit for a frying pan, and some happy reasons exist for putting them there. In the first place, they taste good, especially when filleted and fried in a shallow bath of butter. In the second place, they are such prolific spawners that they often outstrip a pond or lake's ability to keep them well fed. They become stunted. You can help prevent this, and improve the quality of your own fishing, if you keep most of those you catch, take them home, and find your own favorite recipes for cooking them.

Chapter 9

Fly Fishing for Steelhead

Steelhead are the ocean-going variety of the rainbow trout. They hatch from eggs in freshwater streams that have access to saltwater. After one to three years as fry and fingerlings growing at a normal rate for stream trout, they drop down to the ocean, make a far-flung migration of more than 1,000 miles, and balloon into sleek fish weighing from 5 to 25 pounds. When they return to their native streams, after one to four years, they are larger and stronger beyond anything that a stream could produce.

Different runs return to their native waters at different times of the year. Primary runs are in summer and in winter, with minor runs in spring and fall. The different runs react differently to flies, and have to be fished for in different ways.

WINTER STEELHEAD

Fish that enter their native rivers in November or later will spawn soon after arrival. They are reluctant to feed, and rarely move from the bottom to hit a fly. Winter steelhead can be taken with a fly, but only if the fly is delivered right on the bottom, where the fish can react to it without much movement. They will merely intercept it.

SUMMER STEELHEAD

Steelhead that return to their rivers in summer will not spawn until the following spring. They must survive in fresh water through the winter. Therefore they feed more readily than winter fish, to take on some energy. Spring and fall run steelhead also must survive the winter, and like summer fish, are inclined to feed, therefore to tip up and take flies. Most summer steelhead are taken on flies fished just beneath the surface, but they can even be taken on dries.

Summer run steelhead enter their rivers as early as June. Their numbers peak in July and August. They remain in the streams, moving actively, through September and October. July through September is the prime time to fish for them with flies. After the fall rains begin, and the water gets colder, cloudier, and deeper, it becomes much more difficult to entice them up. You've got to go down for them, as you always do for winter fish.

Range and Distribution.

The original range of steelhead was restricted to North Pacific rim waters, from California through Oregon, Washington, British Columbia, Alaska, and down the Russian coast to the Kamchatka Peninsula. A few vigorous runs spend months migrating hundreds of miles inland: to Idaho's Salmon and Clearwater rivers and to British Columbia's central Thompson River.

Steelhead have been transported to Great Lakes rivers, where they use the lakes as their ocean. These have been highly successful transplants. Other steelhead have been transported as far away as southern Chile and New Zealand. Lake Taupo rainbow trout have similar life histories to Great Lakes steelhead, using the lake as their ocean.

skunk

Muddler

Fall Favorite

Winter's Hope

Purple Peril

Boss

FLIES FOR STEELHEAD

Most steelhead flies are designed to fish a few inches to a foot or so beneath the surface. Others float on top for summer steelhead, while a few are designed to sink right to the bottom for winter steelhead. The typical steelhead fly is tied on a #4 or #6 hook. But sizes range from #10 and #12 for low and clear water, up to #2/0 and giant #5/0 for dour winter fish.

Tackle for Steelhead.

Your medium rod will do for summer fish as long as it handles a 6- or 7-weight floating line. Since distance casting is the rule, the rod should be 8½' to 9½' long. For winter fishing, select a heavier rod: an 8- or 9-weight. The reel needs to hold 150 to 200 yards of 20# Dacron backing. It should have a strong and smooth drag.

Most summer fishing can be done with a weight-forward floating line. Back it up with an extra-fast sinking wet-tip for winter fishing. Leaders should be 8' to 10' long, tapered down to tippets that will turn over large flies. That usually means 1X to 3X: from 6# to 15#.

READING STEELHEAD WATER

Summer Steelhead Water.

The best fly water for summer fish is a long run with a current just strong enough to urge you downstream. It should have lots of boulders or ledges to break the current. Fish sprinkle themselves down the length of such water. If it is shallow enough for you to wade, the fish will be willing to move to the top for flies.

When the water gets low, clear, and warm in mid-summer, steelhead tend to hole up in the deepest pools. It's tough to fish for them then. But mornings and evenings they move to the heads and tailouts of pools, and you can take them there.

Winter Steelhead Water.

The difficulty is finding a run suitable for fishing with flies, because you've got to get your fly right to the bottom to move these dour fish. Look for runs of fairly constant depth, usually from 3' to 6'. The bottom should be broken; steelhead will not hold against a current without some shelter. You should be able to wade without danger. If it's too difficult to wade, it's not good fly water.

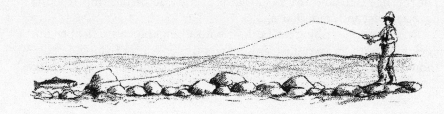

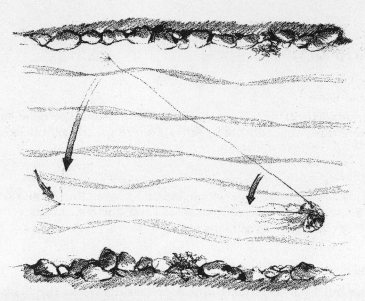

TACTICS FOR STEELHEAD
Damp.

The primary technique for summer steelhead is a fly fished just beneath the surface—damp—on a downstream swing. Wade in at the head of the holding run, cast quartering across the current. Make mends to keep the swing of the fly slow. Fish out each cast until the fly hangs straight below you. Take a couple of steps, then cast again. The technique is the same for waking a dry fly: quarter the cast across and skate it down and around.

Deep.

For winter fish use a weighted fly, or one tied on a heavy hook. If necessary, pinch split shot above the fly. Use a floating line, or a wet-tip if you can't get the fly down. Make short upstream casts. Give the fly time to sink, then fish out its drift while keeping an intent watch on the line tip. If it hesitates or moves upstream, lift the rod to set the hook.

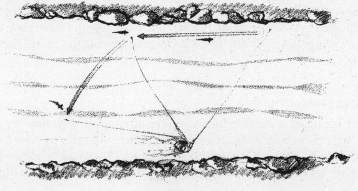

STEELHEAD TIPS

Time of Day.
Steelhead are shy of light. They strike best when the sun is not on the water: dawn and dusk. Your odds are far better if you're up early and out late.

Weather.
A cloudy day, especially one with light rain, enlivens the fish and keeps them active all day. Dawn and dusk are still best, but on such days, you can fish all day with hope of catching some.

Freshets.
If summer fish have been holed up in deep water for weeks, they'll scatter into shallows during and just after the first freshet of early fall. Summer steelheaders enjoy their brightest brief moments.

The Rhythm.
For summer steelhead, never get rooted to one spot. Always take a long step or two between casts. Develop a rhythm as you fish down a run: step and cast, step and cast.

Playing Steelhead.
These are such strong fish that you've got to play them off the reel. Your first goal, when hooking one, is to get all the slack out of the line on the first run. Then play the fish against the drag, never letting it get slack on you.

The Tapping Take.
Often you'll feel little plucks at your fly. It's easy to mistake these for troutlings. They're steelhead. If you feel a tap, make the same cast. If that doesn't bring the fish, switch flies and repeat the cast to achieve the same swing.

Spotting Fish.
When fishing for winter steelhead, you can often spend your time wisely by scouting the river, looking for fish rather than probing for them with your fly. Use binoculars and polarized sunglasses. Once you've located fish, calculate the best approach to get your fly right to them, on the bottom.

Chapter 10
Fly Fishing for Salmon

Salmon leave the egg in freshwater streams and rivers, get a short start there, drop down to the ocean, and thrive to great size. They return to spawn in their native waters, and can be taken on flies.

ATLANTIC SALMON

Atlantic salmon are nearly the perfect fly rod fish. They are large, from 5 to 55 pounds and even larger. They respond to damp flies and floating flies. They are moody, bounding to get flies at times, refusing them at others. Their fight is an aerial astonishment. They return to some of the most beautiful places in the world. It can be very expensive to fish for them.

PACIFIC SALMON

Several species of salmon return to Pacific coastal waters: chinook reach sizes from 15 to 50 pounds; silvers run from 5 to 30 pounds; humpies, sockeye, and dog salmon are lesser fly rod fish that are available only in restricted circumstances. Chinook and silver salmon are more like winter steelhead than like summer steelhead or Atlantic salmon: they do not often move far for flies, and it's best to fish for them near the bottom.

SALMON RANGE AND DISTRIBUTION

Atlantic Salmon Range.

Rivers on the east coast of the United States and Canada have traditional runs of Atlantic salmon. Iceland has many salmon rivers. Russia, all of Scandinavia, and the British Isles have excellent runs. France and Spain still have remnants of runs. Many eastern U. S. runs are now remnants, though efforts are being made to restore them.

Pacific Salmon Range.

The entire arch of the north Pacific is the home range of several salmon species. The west coast from California north through British Columbia and Alaska has heavy runs of both native and hatchery fish. The Siberian rivers of Russia also have excellent salmon runs.

Great Lakes.

Chinook and Pacific salmon have been transplanted to the Great Lakes states, along with steelhead. These fish use the lakes as their ocean, and their runs are now very healthy.

Tackle for Salmon.

Tackle for salmon should be stout. A 9' to 9½' rod balanced to an 8- or 9-weight line will be perfect, and also will turn over the large flies cast for these fish. Buy the best single-action you can afford. It should hold the line plus 200 yards of 20# or 30# Dacron backing, and should have a strong and smooth drag.

In almost all cases a weight-forward floating line will be best. But when fishing deep for Pacific salmon you might add an extra-fast sinking wet-tip. Leaders should be tapered, about the length of the rod or a little longer, heavy enough to turn over large flies, and strong enough to defeat big fish: 8# to 20# test.

Jock Scott

Thunder & Lightning

Bomber

Rusty Rat

Black Bear

Royal Wulff

FLIES FOR SALMON

Flies for Atlantic Salmon.

The most beautiful fly dressings in the world are tied for Atlantic salmon. They have become an art form of their own, though simple flies catch fish just as well. Some are designed to fish on the surface, while others are designed to fish just below it. Sizes range from #3/0 to #10.

Flies for Pacific Salmon.

Flies for Pacific salmon are tied most often to be fished on or near the bottom. Winter steelhead flies serve as well as any. They are typically bright and are often weighted. Pacific salmon often merely mouth a fly, perhaps out of curiosity. Bright flies are visible, and therefore get noticed and taken more often. Sizes are typically #2 to #6.

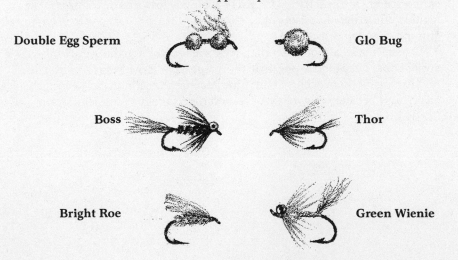

Double Egg Sperm

Glo Bug

Boss

Thor

Bright Roe

Green Wienie

READING SALMON WATER

Atlantic salmon begin to run as early as May. They are in when the water is low and clear, easily fished with flies. Sometimes they school up in the deep pools during hot spells, and become difficult to take. Most of the time they are moving, and can be found in runs and riffles that can be probed with flies.

The best water is 4′ to 10′ deep, of a fairly constant depth and current speed, with plenty of boulders, ledges, and trenches. Many large Atlantic salmon rivers are best fished from a boat slowly lowered downstream by a guide while the client sets up a casting rhythm similar to that used in summer steelheading.

Most Pacific salmon enter their rivers in fall, though there are limited spring runs. They tend to pile up in the deepest pools, waiting for rain. The best fishing for them occurs at this time because the salmon can be located easily, and because they become reluctant to take flies while migrating upstream.

TACTICS FOR SALMON

Damp Swing.

In the damp swing for Atlantic salmon, make the cast long, covering all of the water that you can. Quarter across the current and slightly down. The faster the current, the farther downstream you should cast to slow the swing of the fly. Use constant mends to slow it further. The slower the current, the farther upstream you should place your cast, in order to slightly speed the swing.

Be sure to get into the rhythm of the fishing, taking a step or two between casts. When fishing from a boat, drop a few feet downstream between each series of casts, to cover new water.

Deep Drift.

The deep drift for Pacific salmon calls for casts quartering upstream and across the current. Let the fly settle all the way to the bottom, then be patient while it tumbles along down there. At the end of the drift, let the current lift the fly and the lines; then make your next cast upstream close to the line of drift of the first cast. You've got to cover all of the water very carefully, as these fish will not normally move far for a fly.

Chapter 11
Saltwater Fly Fishing

Saltwater is the latest frontier of fly fishing. Some form of it is available to everybody who lives within striking distance of an ocean coast. Few other branches of fly fishing offer such formidable challenges, or such hefty rewards.

SALTWATER QUARRY

Bonefish and tarpon are found worldwide, wherever inshore shallows abound. Most fishing for them is done in the Florida Keys, off Central America, and around Caribbean islands. Bluefish are also found worldwide, but are pursued most often from the coast of the Carolinas north to inshore New England waters. Caribbean and Baja California waters are full of explosive species such as dorado, barracuda, and roosterfish, all of which can be taken on flies. Bottom fish such as rockfish and lingcod are found most often in estuaries and off the mouths of Pacific coastal rivers.

Bonefish.

These explosive torpedoes are known for a fight that is out of all proportion to their size. They are a fish of shallow inshore waters, and can be best fished for by boating or wading flats. Like all fish in thin water, they are enormously wary. They typically run from 3 to 5 pounds; anything over 7 or 8 pounds is a large fish. When a bonefish takes a fly, it dashes off on powerful runs of 100 yards and sometimes much farther.

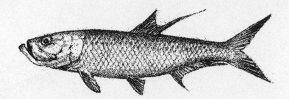

Tarpon.

Among the largest and strongest of fly rod fish, tarpon push weights of 200 pounds, though of course they average half of that. Like bonefish, they cruise shallow flats, and are easily sent to flight, but can be hooked with flies. Their fight is aerial, often high above the boat. It requires the stoutest of tackle to tame them.

Bluefish.

These are migratory deepwater fish that move up the Atlantic shoreline as the water warms in summer. They are astonishingly predatory and aggressive, traveling in schools of same-size fish because any small ones would be gobbled. A fine fish weighs 8 to 15 pounds, and if in a feeding frenzy, will attack any fly with eagerness.

Bottom Fish.

Many species of bottom-dwelling fish become available to fly fishermen where the rocky bottom is not far down. They can be caught on shoals, or along the faces of jetties, especially along the Pacific coast. They include a wide variety of rockfish, lingcod, and perch species, in an equally wide range of shapes and sizes.

FOOD FORMS AND FLIES

A saltwater fly fishing trip involves much thought, cost and preparation. Be sure to consult local sources for recommendations on specific fly patterns. Typical dressings for the salt imitate a variety of food forms that are most abundant in a specific area, and become the most important food source for populations of fish in that area. If your preparations do not include proper fly patterns, you might arrive at a distant and costly destination where it's impossible to get them—and impossible to catch fish without them.

Small crabs are a favorite food for many flats fish. Imitations tied for them should be flat and armed with lots of appendages. Schools of baitfish are the logical prey for such hunters as tarpon and bluefish. Simple streamers, tied on large saltwater hooks, are perfect for them. Many sand and mud flats have prolific populations of shrimp. The most effective bonefish flies bear at least a vague resemblance to them.

TACKLE FOR SALTWATER

Light Saltwater Tackle.

The rod should be 8½' to 9½' long, with a fast action, balanced to a 7- or 8-weight line. The reel should be saltwater-proof, hold the line plus 200 yards of backing, and have an excellent drag. Lines should include a floater in saltwater taper, with most of its weight stacked to the front, plus a special saltwater intermediate. This outfit will be used for casting small flies to bonefish on the flats.

Medium Saltwater Tackle.

An 8½' to 9½' rod that carries a 9- or 10-weight line will help you handle larger flies, and also cast into the teeth of a wind. It will defeat all but the strongest of saltwater fish. The reel should be the best you can afford, holding the line plus 300 yards of backing. Its drag must stop long and strong runs without turning into scraps of metal or emitting wisps of smoke. Lines should include the same saltwater floating and intermediate lines, plus a shooting head system for delivery of longer and quicker casts.

Heavy Saltwater Tackle.

The heavy is for the largest and most brutal species, such as tarpon and billfish. These 8½' to 9½' rods cast 12- to 15-weight lines. Most of their strength is designed to be pitted against the fish, not put into the cast. Reels for this fishing are not only the largest, but also the most expensive because of the ordeals they must endure. In truth, gearing up for any fishing at this level takes you far beyond fly fishing basics. If you're thinking about doing it, invest a lot of time in studying the special literature on saltwater fly fishing before you invest any money at all.

TACTICS FOR FLATS

Any fish venturing into very shallow water must build its life around the constant threat of predation from the skies. Species that feed on saltwater flats have hair triggers and move at blinding speed. That's why it's so difficult to hook a bonefish, and so hard to stop its runs once you do.

Spotting Fish.

Hooking fish on flats depends on seeing them before they see you. Wear clothes that blend with the tans and blues of the shore and the sky. Make no fast or unnecessary movements. Wear polarized glasses and a hat that shields the sun. Watch carefully for fins out of the water, or shadows along the bottom. Expect to spot only a few fish compared to the number that flee from you in alarm.

Presentation.

Carry your rod and line in a position that allows you to cast with minimum movement. Once you've spotted a fish, calculate its direction and speed. Launch the fly with a single backcast; place it 10' to 20' ahead of the fish. Wait until the fish is in range to see the fly. Then begin the retrieve away from the fish, as if the fly is a bait that's escaping.

TACTICS FOR BOTTOM FISH

Saltwater species that live on or near the bottom almost always hover around rocks, which form the perfect retreat. You've got to calculate your cast and retrieve in order to avoid hanging up on the rocks. Once you hook a fish, you've got to force a fight that keeps the fish from finding shelter in the rocks.

Most Pacific coast anglers make up their own lines from 20# or 30# lead core line, cutting off the right length to balance the rod. This is backed with monofilament or fly line for shooting line. The fly is affixed to a short and strong leader. The cast is lobbed out without much delicacy. The countdown method gets the fly to the right depth, just above a shoal or jetty rocks. Use a fast stripping retrieve to keep the fly above the bottom.

Bottom fish hit with a thud. When one does, clamp down on the line, rear back on the rod, and use all the brutality you and your tackle have got to turn the head of the fish. Once you've got it coming, never let up or it will bull into the rocks and break you off.

Chapter 12
Fly Tying Basics

It may seem that the best reason to tie your own flies is the money you save. That's a good reason, but it's not the most important. If you tie your own flies, you are able to tie precisely those flies that you need, matching the food forms that you find most important to your fish. And the flies that you tie, after some practice, will be better quality than flies that you buy.

THE FLY TYING SETUP

It helps to have a tying kit that can be used anywhere; an old briefcase will do. If you've got room, set up a permanent fly tying desk. Protect its top with a sheet of matte paper in light green, which is easy on the eyes. Set a student lamp to shine brightly above your vise.

BASIC TOOLS

A few basic tools are critical. Buy good ones. The *vise* should be adjustable for height and have firm locking jaws. The *scissors* should have straight blades and fine points. The *bobbin* should be adjustable for tension on the thread spool, and have a smooth barrel. The *hackle pliers* need to grip the hackle tip firmly, but not cut it. The *whip finisher* must come with detailed directions that explain how to use it. The *head cement needle* can be as simple as a pin whipped to a matchstick.

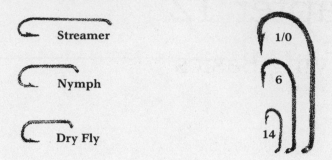

FLY TYING TOOLS

Hooks come in various diameters: 1X fine or 1X heavy means it is the same diameter as the wire for a hook one size smaller or one size larger. A hook 1X long or 1X short is the shank length of a hook one size larger or smaller. Hooks are numbered from #1 to #28; the larger the number the smaller the hook. From #1/0 up to #5/0 and larger, the hook gets larger as its number gets larger.

Dry fly hooks are normally 1X fine, standard length. Nymph hooks are typically 1X long, 2X heavy. Streamer hooks are usually 3X to 4X long, standard weight.

Fly Tying Materials.

Different kinds of flies have different requirements to achieve a life-like look. When tying dry flies, for example, you've got to choose water-repellant furs for the body, and stiff feathers for the hackles, or you'll wind up with dries that are wet and soggy. For nymphs and wets, on the opposite hand, you need materials that attract water, soak it up, sink the fly, and make it look alive beneath the water.

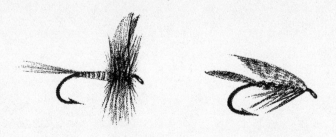

TYING DRY FLIES

Your first purchase when beginning to tie flies should be a pattern book. The materials in a good book will be listed in the order in which you tie them onto the hook. The following is the sequence for tying a typical dry fly.

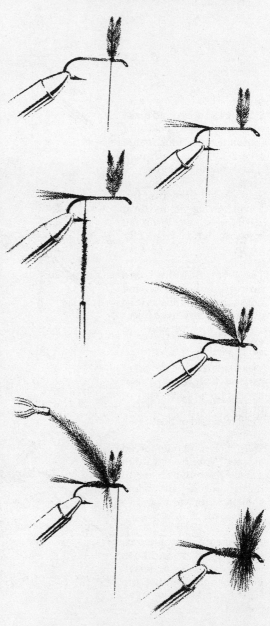

Step 1.
Fix thread onto hook with 5 overlapping turns. Choose two hackle tips, measure length of hook shank, tie in with tips forward. 8-10 turns of thread in front stand them up.

Step 2.
Select 8-12 stiff hackle fibers. Measure the length of hook shank. Tie in with 5 firm turns of thread, then wind thread to base of wing butts and clip excess tail.

Step 3.
Twist body dubbing fur onto thread. Use thumb and forefinger of one hand and twist in only one direction, until fur is a tight rope.

Step 4.
Wind dubbing forward in neatly tapered body. Leave 1/16" gap behind the wing, for hackle. Tie in one rooster hackle, with fibers the length of hook shank, just behind the wing.

Step 5.
Grip tip of hackle with pliers and take first turn at end of body. Wrap 3-4 turns of hackle behind wing, 2-3 turns in front of wing.

Step 6.
Tie off hackle tip with 4-5 turns of thread. Clip excess hackle. Use minimum number of thread turns to form neat tapered head. Use whip finisher to tie off. Clip thread, apply lead cement.

TYING NYMPHS

Nymphs are as varied in form as natural insect nymphs, larvae, pupae, crustaceans, and myriad other forms. But learn the basics and you can vary the imitation to fit the natural.

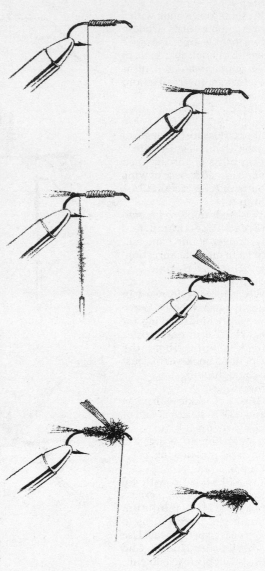

Step 1.
Start thread at eye and make layer to tail. Select lead wire the diameter of hook shank, take 8-12 turns with it in middle of the hook.

Step 2.
Select long fibers from fur, or soft hen hackle, and tie in at end of shank. Wrap tail butts to lead wire, clip excess.

Step 3.
Twist fur dubbing onto thread, leaving it looser and not such a tight rope as for a dry fly, so it will have fibers sticking out to work in water.

Step 4.
Wrap tapered body to point just forward of mid-point of hook. Clip ⅛" to ¼" strip of turkey quill for shellback. Tie it in at end of body.

Step 5.
Twist thorax fur onto thread loosely. Wrap it forward to hook eye, but be sure to leave room to bring shellback forward, and to make head.

Step 6.
Draw shellback over thorax, and tie it off behind hook eye. Clip excess material. Form a neat head, whip finish, and apply head cement.

TYING WET FLIES

Wet flies should look alive and kicking in the water. Tie them with loose-fibered bodies and hen feathers for wings, and all of their parts will wobble when tugged by the currents.

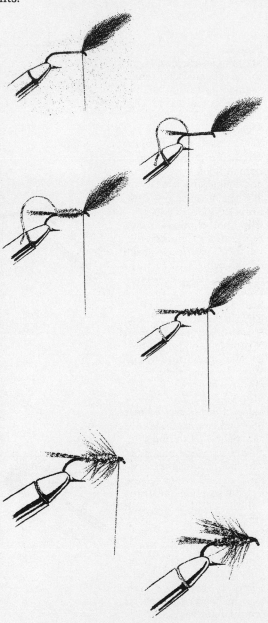

Step 1.
Select a hen hackle with fibers the length of the hook shank. Tie it in with concave side away from hook shank, so hackle will sweep back when fly is finished.

Step 2.
Tie in tail of 3-6 hen hackle fibers, the length of the hook shank. Tie in 3"-4" of ribbing wire or tinsel at base of tail.

Step 3.
Twist dubbing fur loosely onto thread and wind tapered body to base of hackle. Be sure to leave room for wing and for hook eye.

Step 4.
Wind rib to end of body in 3-5 evenly spaced turns. Tie it down with 3 turns of thread, then double tinsel back and lock it in with 3 more turns.

Step 5.
Move thread one-third of way back on body. Take 2 turns of hackle at front, then 2 more turns spaced back to thread. Tie and clip there, then wind thread through hackle back to hook eye.

Step 6.
Clip 2 wing segments, 1/8" to 1/4" thick, from matched mallard wing feathers. Meld together, and tie in by drawing thread straight down, to keep them from rolling over. Clip excess, form neat head, whip finish, and cement.

TYING STREAMERS

Streamers usually are tied to look like some form of baitfish. One of the most effective streamers of all time is the Muddler Minnow, shown here.

Step 1.
Start thread at eye and wind to end of shank. Clip a small segment of turkey tail and tie it in as tail. Tie 4"-5" of tinsel in for the body.

Step 2.
Wind tinsel in overlapping turns to a point ¼" or so behind hook eye. Tie it off and double it back to tie it off again before clipping excess.

Step 3.
Clip small clump of brown bucktail for underwing. Even the tips. Tie it in at end of body with 6-10 firm turns of thread. Clip excess on taper.

Step 4.
Clip single section ¼" or so from turkey tail feather. Measure it to end of tail, tie it in over the underwing. Wind it down tightly and clip excess.

Step 5.
Select clump of hollow deer body hair about the size of a lead pencil. Clip from skin, clean fuzz from butts. Hold it to hook shank, take 2 loose turns around it, then release it while pulling the turns tight. It will flare and spin around hook.

Step 6.
If needed, spin one more clump of deer hair. Whip finish and clip thread. Use scissors or sharp razor blade to trim head into tapered sculpin-like shape.

TYING HAIR BUGS

Hair bugs are among the most deadly lures for bass and panfish. The method in tying them is the same as that used for the Muddler Head: spun deer hair trimmed to shape.

Step 1.
Start thread at the bend of the hook, leaving the rest of the shank bare. Tie in a feather tail and clip the excess close to the tie-in point.

Step 2.
Clip a pencil-sized patch of hollow deer hair. Clean fuzz from the butts. Hold hair at base of tail and take 2 loose turns around it.

Step 3.
Release the hair clump and at the same time pull the thread tight. The hair will flare and spin around the entire hook shank. Use thumb and forefinger to pack it tightly back toward the tail.

Step 4.
Clip and clean another hair clump. It can be a different color, resulting in a prettier bug. Spin it as in Steps 2 and 3, and pack it back.

Step 5.
On a small hook, 2 deer hair clumps might finish the fly. On a larger hook, add 1 more clump behind the hook eye, spinning it as before. It can be the color of the first, giving a segmented bug.

Step 6.
Whip finish and clip thread. Use your scissors or razor to trim the bug to shape. Start by clipping it flat on the bottom, then taper rest of body.

TYING STEELHEAD AND SALMON FLIES

Tying complicated Atlantic salmon flies is truly an art. But you're best off beginning with a simple hairwing dressing such as the Black Bear for salmon or the Skunk for steelhead.

Step 1.
Fix thread to hook behind eye. Measure a clump of bucktail, calftail, or foxtail the length of the hook shank. Tie in with tips over eye of hook. Clip butts.

Step 2.
Measure hackle fiber tail the length of one and one-half hook gaps, and tie in. Tie body chenille at base of tail, then ribbing tinsel. Fur can also be used for body.

Step 3.
Wind body material forward, but leave gap behind wing butts. Tie off. Bring rib forward in 4-5 even turns. Tie off by doubling over itself.

Step 4.
Select soft rooster or hen hackle with fibers the length of the tail: equal to 2 hook gaps. Tie it in between the wing butts and the end of the body.

Step 5.
Wing 4-5 turns of hackle behind the wing, ahead of the body. Tie off and clip tip. Wind thread through hackle 4-5 times, to lock it in.

Step 6.
Draw wing back over body of fly with thumb and forefinger. Take wraps up over base until wing stands up at 30- to 45-degree angle. Finish neat head. Whip finish twice, and use 3-4 coats of head cement.

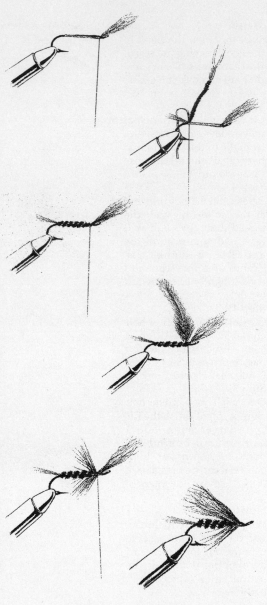

TYING SALTWATER FLIES

The Lefty's Deceiver, designed by noted fly fishing author Lefty Kreh, is perhaps the best saltwater fly to practice on. It's easy to tie, it is widely effective, and it can be tied in a rainbow of colors and still catch fish.

Step 1.
Select 6-8 saddle hackle feathers. Place them back to back so when tied on they'll flare outward. Tie them in and wrap the butts two-thirds the length of the hook shank.

Step 2.
Tie in 6-10 strips of narrow tinsel slightly shorter than the tails, for flash. Tie in 4"-6" of wide tinsel for the body.

Step 3.
Wrap the body tinsel forward to a point one-third of the hook shank length behind the eye. Be sure to double it over when tying it off, to lock it in.

Step 4.
Tie in a bucktail collar at the end of the body, the length of the shank. Use loose loops to tie it in and spread it evenly around the hook shank.

Step 5.
Tie in an overwing, using bucktail a different color than the underwing. Do not spread it around the hook but leave it just on the top of the fly.

Step 6.
Add a few peacock herls for topping. Tie them off, and wind a large head on the fly. Whip finish it at least twice, and use 3-4 coats of head cement. Paint eyes on the head if you'd like.

Bibliography

Bashline, L. James. *Atlantic Salmon Fishing.* Harrisburg: Stackpole Books, 1987.

Brooks, Charles E. *Nymph Fishing for Larger Trout.* New York: Lyons & Burford, 1976.

Combs, Trey. *Steelhead Fly Fishing and Flies.* Portland: Frank Amato Publications, 1976.

Ferguson, Bruce, Les Johnson, and Pat Trotter. *Fly Fishing for Pacific Salmon.*
   Portland: Frank Amato Publications, 1985.

Hughes, Dave. *Handbook of Hatches.* Harrisburg: Stackpole Books, 1986.
   Reading the Water. Harrisburg: Stackpole Books, 1987.
   Tackle & Technique for Taking Trout. Harrisburg: Stackpole Books, 1988.
   Tactics for Trout. Harrisburg: Stackpole Books, 1990.
   Strategies for Stillwater. Harrisburg: Stackpole Books, 1991.
   American Fly Tying Manual. Portland: Frank Amato Publications, 1986.

Humphreys, Joe. *Joe Humphreys's Trout Tactics* (second edition).
   Harrisburg: Stackpole Books, 1993.

Kreh, Lefty. *Fly Fishing in Salt Water.* New York: Lyons & Burford, 1986.

Leisenring, James and Vernon S. Hidy. *The Art of Tying the Wet Fly.* New York: Dodd, Mead & Company, 1941.

McClane, A. J. *McClane's Standard Fishing Encyclopedia.* New York: Holt, Rinehart and Winston, 1965.

Meyer, Deke. *Advanced Fly Fishing for Steelhead.* Portland: Frank Amato Publications, 1992.

Murray, Harry. *Fly Fishing for Smallmouth Bass.* New York: Nick Lyons Books, 1989.

Nemes, Sylvester. *The Soft-Hackled Fly.* Harrisburg: Stackpole Books, 1993

Schnell, Judith and Judith Stolz. *Trout.* Harrisburg: Stackpole Books, 1991.

Sosin, Mark and Lefty Kreh. *Practical Fishing Knots II.* New York: Lyons & Burford, 1972.

Talleur, Dick. *Mastering the Art of Fly Tying.* Harrisburg: Stackpole Books, 1979.